HEARTLAND
OF THE MIDDLE EAST

Discovering the Impact of
Buddhism, Christianity & Islam

A Travel Journal

By B.L. Turner

Heartland of the Middle East: Discovering the Impact of Buddhism, Islam & Christianity, A Travel Journal

© 2022, 2023 by B.L. Turner. All rights reserved.

Fig Press
3631 NE 102nd Ave
Portland, OR 97220

ISBN: 978-1-961528-04-8
Ebook ISBN: 978-1-961528-05-5

Unless otherwise indicated, all Scripture quotations are from the American Standard Version (ASV). Quotations from other translations are indicated by three-letter identifiers and are copyrighted by their respective publishers.

Photos were taken and copyrighted by B.L. Turner or Jonathan Turner, unless otherwise noted. All rights reserved.

Dedication

With great joy and gratitude, I dedicate this book to the memory of

Nellie E. Copley.

From her total dedication to the cause of Christ

she committed a significant portion of her time, energy and resources,

supplementing those of other dedicated followers of Christ,

to make our fifteen-year ministry in Pakistan possible.

Acknowledgment

Thank you to my son, Jonathan Turner, for the many, many hours he spent drawing original maps to go with these letters and text. I am grateful to him for his help with locating photos out of a thousand slides that we took.

Not only that, but I am thankful Jonathan was able to go on this journey with me, providing encouraging companionship, as well as being an excellent mechanic and a first-class navigator. It was a father-son trip like no other!

TABLE OF CONTENTS

Preface..1

Introduction..3

Chapter 1: Background: Christianity in the Center Arena......................9

Chapter 2: The Setting: Afghanistan..17

Chapter 3: The Silk Road: Letter No. 1..25

Chapter 4: The Giant Buddhas: Letter No. 2......................................33

Chapter 5: Alexandria of the East: Letter No. 3..................................41

Chapter 6: Slaves to Conquerors: Letter No. 4...................................45

Chapter 7: Glimpses of Afghan Life...53

Chapter 8: The Setting: Iran...61

Chapter 9: The Threshold of Asian Modernity: Letter No. 5................67

Chapter 10: On the Way to Tehran: Letter No. 6................................73

Chapter 11: Half the World: Letter No. 7...81

Chapter 12: World Capitals: Letter No. 8...93

Chapter 13: Background: Turkey...115

Chapter 14: Esther & Mordecai: Letter No. 9...................................119

Chapter 15: In Abraham's Steps: Letter No. 10................................127

Chapter 16: They Loved Not Their Life: Letter No. 11.......................133

Chapter 17: Entrepots in the Desert: Letter No. 12 137

Chapter 18: East of Jordan & Aqaba: Letter No. 13..........................145

Chapter 19: John & Moses Called Home: Letter No. 14....................161

Table of Contents, Continued

Chapter 20: A Cosmopolitan City for a Cosmopolitan Gospel: Letter No. 15..163

Epilogue..169

Atlas..171
    Area of Travel..171
    Pakistan..172
    Afghanistan..173
    Iran..174
    Syria..175
    Turkey...176
    Jordan...177
    Turkish Waterways..178

Alphabetical Index...179

About the Author..197

Preface

It is appropriate to explain why several years after making an extensive trip through western Asia and the Middle East, the travel letters written during that journey are only now being published.

At the time these letters were written, copies were mailed only to family and a few close friends. However, they are not casual letters discussing only ephemeral or trivial matters. Rather, they discuss matters of enduring importance. They touch issues of deepest interest, not only to Christians concerned with the current progress of Gospel outreach in the area of focus but also to many others who seek to understand some of the most fundamental issues and developments of our times.

These letters, along with accurate maps, appended notes, commentaries, and many accompanying photographs, offer rewarding source material in addition to pleasurable reading. This is especially so for students of the geography and history of the eastern Bible lands, as well as to students of Christian missions and church history. Doubtless, beyond students focusing on those areas, there will be many others who will find these letters of great interest because of the insight they offer, not only to the Bible lands, but to developments in the past, the present, and clues to future developments.

Events in the intervening years since Jonathan and I began our odyssey have made the topics of these letters even more vital and relevant: (1) The inexorable drive of the Russian Empire to the south advanced a major new step with its fruitless invasion (beginning on Christmas day 1979) and partial but brief occupation of Afghanistan. (2) The overthrow of the Shah of Iran, (3) the ongoing bloody Iranian revolution initiated under Imam Khomeini in 1979 and carried on by his successors, and (4) the prolonged war which took place between Iran and Iraq before Khomeini's death, were some of the major convulsions. Their full outcome will ultimately touch all of us in basic and important ways. These letters help put those events, as well as the continuing Palestinian-Israeli struggle and the Super Power confrontation in the Middle and Far East and in western Asia, in better perspective.

In addition to those important contributions, these letters, along with commentary, will be enjoyable reading for many as they travel with Jonathan and me through one of the most fascinating and vital areas of the biblical and modern world.

§

Heartland of the Middle East

Introduction

My attention was originally attracted to the whole world of Islam in 1946, in a church history class at San Jose Bible College, where I heard of Islam for the first time. As I read of the common ground existing between Islam and Christianity I failed to understand why our voluntary fellowship of churches, aspiring to follow the biblical pattern, was sending no one to work among Muslim people. After all, Muslims believed in the one God who created heaven and earth. They believed the Bible was (originally at least) a divinely inspired book. They believed Jesus of Nazareth (though the son of the Virgin Mary but not the Son of God) was a unique prophet sent from God. My astonished remark in the midst of our class, upon hearing all this, took the form of a question directed to my professor. I asked, "Since these people are so close to us, why aren't we helping them cross the threshold?" That question never received an answer which I deemed to have been even remotely satisfactory.

About seven years later, James A. Michener, in an electrifying article entitled "*Pakistan, Divided It Stands,*" (*Reader's Digest*, November 1954) riveted my attention on Pakistan which was at that time the world's largest Muslim country. Today, based on population, it is the world's fifth largest country. It continued to be the world's largest Muslim country until 1971 when, by civil war, East Pakistan became independent as Bangladesh. During those seven years between my first introduction to Islam and Michener's monograph, I had read, among other missionary literature, John R. Mott's highly motivating, The Evangelization of the World in This Generation. Also, I had been teaching for four years in a church college which had evangelism as its focal point. I deeply felt I couldn't ask young men and women to prepare for work I would not be willing to do myself. I was, therefore, ready to say with Isaiah, (with these reservations: if my personality, if my abilities, if my understanding may be of any use) "Here am I, send me." (Isaiah 6:8)

Because Gerry, my loving and godly wife, concurred with my personal desire to gain the necessary skills, I began preparing myself for service in Pakistan to share the message of Jesus Christ. Those efforts led me to the South Asia Regional Studies Program at the University of Pennsylvania. During those studies, I began a personal inquiry into the origins and status of Christianity, particularly in that part of the Muslim world which stretches westward from the Indus River Valley in Pakistan to the Mediterranean. That inquiry, I thought, should be made from as broad a perspective as possible. Partly to gain that perspective, my Master's Thesis was, "A Contribution to the English Historical Cartography of Iran in the Early Islamic Period." Among other emphases, that thesis discussed the "Distribution of Islamic and Non-Islamic Religions in Iran in Early Islamic Times." Hoping to visit Iran, which was highlighted in my thesis, along with other Middle Eastern Muslim countries, I, along with Jonathan, our youngest son, who shared this exploratory trip with me, made many preparations to make our discovery trip possible. Our resulting odyssey was described in the series of letters which constitute the heart of this book.

Because our inquiry concerned only the area from the Indus River to the Mediterranean, the Homeward-Bound Letters only take the reader to Antioch, Apamea, Latakia, and Ras Shamra/Ugarit in the west.

Previously, in 1965, I had wanted to make a similar "voyage" of discovery with David, our oldest son. We had hoped to buy a couple of motorcycles for transportation, but that dream proved to be completely beyond our financial means. However, the dream persisted, and as I spoke of it with Jonathan, our youngest son, he began to dream with me. Our over-20-year-old Jeep station wagon would have to be completely renovated if we would have any reasonable hope of getting all the way through. Jonathan completely dismantled the Jeep and rebuilt it from the frame up! (The mechanical troubles we had en route did not originate from his fine work but from inaccurate information about a clutch plate and a factory mistake in a bearing in the replacement engine.) While I am the actual writer of the letters, Jonathan made a tremendous contribution to the expedition at every stage. It was his odyssey as much as mine. Both of us look back, not only to a fascinating time of discovery and insight, but to six months of tremendous camaraderie between father and son.

Throughout Afghanistan, Transport Experiences an Epochal Change

In all the centuries during which the Silk Road was the exclusive land route of transport between the Far East, the Middle East and Europe, animals provided the only means by which inland travel and carriage of goods took place. The development of the steam engine and the internal combustion engine would ultimately displace animals from their exclusive role in the carriage trade and in human transport. However, those developments took centuries to be completed. The extended period of overlap between animal-based and machine-based transport was often picturesque. While Jonathan and I had experienced such an ongoing transition period in our years of residence in Pakistan, we found the comparable

On the roads in Afghanistan, roles may be reversed! A sick camel gets a ride for medical treatment!

Introduction

period in Afghanistan, which was in development as we began our tour of the Middle East, to be arresting! These two photos will help you savor the nostalgia as one era ends and its replacement dawns.

This was our Jeep! Though motor roads now connect most of the major population centers in Afghanistan, the roads must accommodate multiple use. Automotive traffic must yield right-of-way to camel caravans which still carried cargo that was economically significant in the Afghan economy.

Except for current event updates, these travel letters have remained just as I wrote them during the trip. Of course, spellings have been corrected and, in one case, I deleted a personal name for a person's safety. Also, I tell for the first time that it was an Iranian army convoy stalled on the snow-clogged pass between Hamadan and Kermanshah.

Reasonably, someone may wonder how these letters of travel could have been as well-documented as they were while we were traveling. We carried a sizable library with us in a bookcase built into the Jeep, supplemented by many more books in the roof rack. The appropriate volumes for any given segment of the trip were kept out of the case and when they weren't being studied were used to level the surface in the back of the Jeep where we spread our sleeping bags. Periodically we would "hole-up" in some very cheap hotel or campground so we not only could do our laundry, but so I could turn my rough notes into readable letters.

Our trip to explore the Middle East began on October 3, 1975, just a few minutes before sundown when the Torkham border crossing between Pakistan and Afghanistan would close. In Lahore, Pakistan, I had been translating B.S. Dean's <u>Outline of Bible History</u> from English to Urdu in order to publish it in Pakistan. In order to finish that work, I had applied for an extension six times for a further stay in Lahore. The last time, the police officer with whom I dealt said, "Mr. Turner, I have extended your stay in Pakistan for as long as I have authorization to do it." So, we left Lahore, but on our way to Rawalpindi, we realized that the rubber-mounted suspension system on our small trailer was not strong enough. Fortunately, in Rawalpindi, I was able to get a three-day further extension of our stay in order to put regular steel springs in the suspension system of the trailer.

This is the Pakistani gate through which one crosses into Afghanistan at the Torkam border. (Jonathan at right.)

Finishing that work, we made our way to Peshawar, the nearest northern Pakistani city close to the famous Torkham Border Crossing into Afghanistan. We were required to cross by sundown.

On the way to the border, two astounding roadside archaeological artifacts forcefully reminded us that the area now known as Pakistan was not always dominated by Islam. Just east of the Grand Trunk Road, by which we were making our way north to Rawalpindi and on to Peshawar, a few miles beyond Gujranwala, is a striking remnant of the once powerful Buddhist civilization. Centuries earlier, Buddhism had broken the power of Hinduism. Previously, Hinduism had gained the allegiance of the vast majority of people in the enormous area from the Bay of Bengal to the western border of the Indus River valley.

Subsequently, Buddhism triumphed over Hinduism in the area now occupied by Pakistan. Here, the ruins of magnificent, many-centuries-old, Buddhist stupas portray, beyond the ability of verbal description or explanation, the power of Buddhism.

This photo of the stupa near Gujranwala, Pakistan was taken several years after Jonathan and I began our travels through the countries lying between Pakistan's Indus River and the Mediterranean Sea.

Introduction

In addition to the unmistakable testimony of these stupas, it is clear that Buddhism was once a very powerful ideology, triumphing over the entire length of the Indus River. When Muslim forces, following the sea coast, came from the west in their compassionless military campaign to the Indus River and then north all the way to the city of Multan, they found Buddhism to be completely dominant in that entire area.

By his teaching, Gautama Buddha successfully challenged the Hindu doctrine of perpetual reincarnation. According to that concept, at death the spirit of the departed person was reincarnated in some animal or insect form until, through proper use of his greatly limited new ability, he earned his way up to the next higher level of existence. In comparison, the Roman Catholic doctrine of purgatory seems almost benign!

Having conceptually triumphed over Hinduism's doctrine of reincarnation, Buddhism embraced four noble truths and an eight-fold noble path. The truths are: 1) The definition of sorrow; 2) The cause of sorrow; 3) Stopping sorrow; 4) The path of victory over sorrow. Then the convert committed himself/herself to tread an eight-fold noble path embracing right views, right resolve, right speech, right conduct (embracing pacifism, that is, no harm to living beings), right livelihood, right effort, right recollection and right meditation.

Though there are ruins of many comparatively minor ancient Buddhist stupas still to be seen in several areas of northern Pakistan, the stunning impact of the great stupa, just northeast of Gujranwala, is powerfully accentuated by another enormous stupa constructed on a roadside hilltop which one may see shortly before reaching Peshawar from Rawalpindi [see picture to the left]. Our second travel letter will show that Buddhism also came, with even greater power, into northern Afghanistan.

A stupa is a structure in which a priceless, revered artifact from the Buddha is enshrined in a beautiful container designed to protect it for centuries. Buddhist worshipers show their devotion to the Buddha and his teaching by walking worshipfully around the stupa a prescribed number of times. Often, the artifact was only a tuft of hair from the scalp of the Buddha.

Just a few minutes before the time limit would have expired, we crossed the border into Afghanistan and I wept, both in sorrow and in thanksgiving. I felt great sorrow in ending a 15-year residence in Pakistan. I had to bid good-bye to many dear friends and to realize that my resident ongoing Christian work in that country had come to a close.

Heartland of the Middle East

We prayed at that border crossing, with tears, to thank God for the 15 years he had given us in Pakistan and for the beginning of a new segment of our lives. These *Homeward Bound Letters* began with that prayer.

§

Chapter 1

Background: Christianity in the Center Arena

What were the origins of Christianity in this crucial area which I call the center arena of history? The beginning of the church in Egypt, Palestine, Syria, and in the areas to the west which are situated north of the Mediterranean, is reasonably well-known because of the captivating record in the Book of Acts and the New Testament Epistles. However, there is no comparable New Testament documentation for the origin of the church in the countries lying between Palestine and the Indus Valley (or for that matter, all the way to the Bay of Bengal or even further east). That makes the problem of historical clarity in those areas more difficult. Existing non-biblical historical sources are meager. However, the reason for the scarcity of source materials is well-known. "From the third century there were long periods of persecution which involved the ruthless destruction of churches and monastic institutions and other depositories of invaluable historical documents."[1]

The destruction of churches is confirmed even by Muslim authors. For example, the Muslim writer Ibn Hauqal (Hawkal) gives graphic confirmation of this when he mentions that, in the 10th century A.D. Barki (modern Mekeh) in the Syr River watershed, known anciently as the Jaxartes River, now in southern Russia had a "Friday mosque that had originally been a (Nestorian) Christian church."[2] As I note later, there was also a church in Seistan (Sistan), Afghanistan. However, when the Mongol Timur (Tamerlane) appeared there with his ruthless hordes, "the capital of Sistan closed its gates, and declined to surrender. After a short siege it was taken by storm, all its inhabitants who could be found were massacred, its walls were then razed and its houses destroyed. Since that time Zaranj [capital of Seistan] has come to be a nameless ruin."[3]

Still, we are not totally without clues to the past. As Christy Wilson pointed out in his fascinating book about the contemporary Christian situation in Afghanistan, the "crosses, still woven in Afghan carpets, witness to the past Christian era,[4] and old coins bore the legend 'In the name of the Father, Son, and Holy Ghost, one God.'"[5]

There are even more intriguing clues. "According to two ancient historians, Eusebius (c. A.D. 260-340) and Socrates (c. A.D. 380-450), the twelve apostles parceled among themselves missionary responsibility for the [then] known world. Thomas was assigned to the Parthian Empire, and India, with Bartholomew sharing in the latter area of mission."[6]

There is very strong presumptive evidence that Thomas fulfilled his commission. In an ancient document entitled *The Acts of Saint Thomas*, long thought by competent scholars to be completely spurious, we are told that Thomas preached the Gospel to King Gondophares who accepted Christ. Since many of the sermons attributed to Thomas in that document are Manichaean propaganda forgeries, it was thought that the story of the conversion of Gondophares was nothing more than fiction. After all, no one had previously ever heard of such a king outside of that reference![7] However, when Taxila (about 25 miles west of Rawalpindi, Pakistan) was excavated, hordes of coins minted by King Gondophares came to light! Also, "long before any coins or inscriptions of Gondophares had been discovered, the name was known to the Western world in connexion with the Mission of St. Thomas in India."[8] But with the discovery of the Taxila coins it was realized that not everything in *The Acts of Saint Thomas* was spurious after all! The best scholarly estimate is that the historical and geographical matters in *The Acts* are reliable. Many of the sermons and discourses of Thomas were probably forged by the Manichaeans in the only extant copies of the document in order to get their views accepted by the Christians who were then numerous in the area. This is a testimony that in apostolic times the Gospel not only had come to what is now northwest Pakistan but that Christians in the whole area from the Euphrates (the center of Manichaeism was on the lower Euphrates) to the Indus Valley were numerous enough that the Manichaeans wanted to proselytize them!

Strength of Christianity

There is evidence that Christianity in pre-Islamic times was significantly present in the area stretching from the Indus River in Pakistan to the Orontes River in Syria. While this was well-known in reference to the Mediterranean littoral, it applies also to the arena now comprising Iran, Afghanistan and Pakistan. One comes to this conclusion, first, because it seems to have obliged Buddhism to alter its doctrine. The form of Buddhism known as Mahayana Buddhism arose in the area stretching from Rawalpindi, Pakistan to Bamiyan, Afghanistan. In the concept of Mahayana Buddhism, which is an abrupt and radical departure from the much older Hinayana form, surviving in Sri Lanka (Ceylon), man needs a savior. The savior in this case is the one who has achieved the right to join those in Nirvana, such a one is called a Bodhisattva, but voluntarily refuses entrance to that state of bliss in order to suffer on behalf of others so they, too, may be "saved." A.L. Basham makes a very profound analysis about the origin of this theological change.[9] In his great work, <u>The Wonder That Was India</u>, he says, "the suffering Bodhisattva so closely resembles the Christian conception of the God who gives his life as a ransom for many that we cannot dismiss the possibility that the doctrine was borrowed by Buddhism from Christianity, which was vigorous in Persia from the 3rd century A.D. onwards."[10] It should be kept in mind that Persia at the time to which Basham refers included what is now Afghanistan and Pakistan.

But why should Buddhism in what is now northern Pakistan and Afghanistan want to borrow a radically new theology from Christianity? The best answer is, to compete with Christianity, the new faith that was winning many converts from

Chapter 1~Background: Christianity in the Center Arena

Buddhism in that very area! That dramatic doctrinal difference was captured in an immortal poem by R. T. H. Griffith. He expressed that timeless clash by unforgettable verses in his poem, *The Suppliant Dove*, in which he wrote:

> *Chased by a hawk, there came a dove*
> *With worn and weary wing,*
> *And took her stand upon the hand*
> *Of Kasi's noble king.*
>
> *The monarch smoothed her ruffled plumes.*
> *And laid her on his breast;*
> *And cried, "No fear shall vex thee here,*
> *Rest, pretty egg-born, rest!*
>
> *Fair Kasi's realm is rich and wide,*
> *With golden harvests gay,*
> *But all that's mine will I resign*
> *Ere I my guest betray."*
>
> *But, panting for his half-won spoil,*
> *The hawk was close behind.*
> *And with wild eye and eager cry*
> *Came swooping down the wind:*
>
> *"This bird," he cried, "my destined prize,*
> *'Tis not for thee to shield:*
> *'Tis mine by right and toilsome flight*
> *O'er hill and dale and field.*
>
> *Hunger and thirst oppress me sore.*
> *And I am faint with toil:*
> *Thou should'st not stay a bird of prey.*
> *Who claims his rightful spoil.*
>
> *They say thou art a glorious king,*
> *And justice is thy care;*
> *Then justly reign in thy domain,*
> *Nor rob the birds of air."*
>
> *Then cried the king: "A cow or deer*
> *For thee shall straightway bleed,*

Heartland of the Middle East

*Or let a ram or tender lamb
Be slain, for thee to feed.*

*Mine oath forbids me to betray
My little twice-born guest:
See, how she clings, with trembling wings.
To her protector's breast."*

*"No flesh of lambs," the hawk replied,
"No blood of deer for me;
The falcon loves to feed on doves.
And such is Heaven's decree.*

*But if affection for the dove
Thy pitying heart has stirred,
Let thine own flesh my maw refresh,
Weighed down against the bird."*

*He carved the flesh from off his side.
And threw it in the scale.
While women's cries smote on the skies
With loud lament and wail.*

*He hacked the flesh from side and arm,
From chest and back and thigh,
But still above the little dove
The monarch's scale stood high.*

*He heaped the scale with piles of flesh.
With sinews, blood, and skin.
And when alone was left him bone
He threw himself therein.*

*Then thundered voices through the air;
The sky grew black as night;
And fever took the earth that shook
To see that wondrous sight.*

*The blessed Gods, from every sphere,
By Indra led, came nigh;
While drum and flute and shell and lute
Made music in the sky.*

Chapter 1~Background: Christianity in the Center Arena

They rained immortal chaplets down,
Which hands celestial twine,
And softly shed upon his head
Pure Amrit, drink divine.

Then God and Seraph, Bard and Nymph
Their heavenly voices raised.
And a glad throng with dance and song
The glorious monarch praised.

They set him on a golden car
That blazed with many a gem;
Then swiftly through the air they flew.
And bore him home with them.

Thus Kasi's lord, by noble deed,
Won Heaven and deathless fame;
And when the weak protection seek
From thee, do thou the same.

Enshrined in Griffith's incomparable poem are unmistakable, unique gospel concepts: the concept of divine justice, of God protecting those who seek him, and finally, of the ultimate sacrifice of the Saviour himself—all reflecting the values being preached in the Gospel of Christ. As a message to Hindus, and all who follow their precepts, they are told that gods from "every sphere by Indra led, came nigh." What a powerful message, that the deities of Hinduism bow in reverence to the suffering Savior! In view of these and other remarkable parallels between the poem and the Gospel, it is not surprising that the message of Christ was notably successful in the area that we today call Afghanistan.

As thrilling as the inferential evidence from the accounts of Thomas and the Mahayana Buddhists is, we can be still more specific: the Muslim traveler and geographer, Ab-ul-Qasim Muhammad Ibn Hauqal (Hawkal),[11] "tells of a Christian church in [the famous Afghan city of] Herat, but makes only slight mention of Christianity in Samercand; yet we know both from Albyrouny's [born ca. A.D. 971] language (Chron. of Ancient Nations, p. 282 in Sachau's E. tr.) as well as from the Nestorian funeral inscriptions lately discovered in the Semiretchi or district of the seven rivers, that Christianity had many followers in Central Asia beyond the Oxus [River] at this very time."[12]

Also, Ibn Hauqal (Hawkal) records that in the hills some "two leagues" north of Herat in the 10th century A.D. was a fire temple "called Sirishk. ... A Christian church also stood at a place lying halfway between this fire temple and the city."[13]

A bishop for the Christians on both sides of the Amu River, previously known as the Oxus River, was sent by the Nestorian Patriarch in 549 A.D.[14] Because records of early Christianity in the area have been largely destroyed, as has already been stressed, knowledge of the church in what is now Afghanistan comes mostly through intriguing historical vignettes. However, from the writings of the patriarch Jesu-Jabus, about 650 A.D., it is clear that there was a church in Balkh and enough Christians "in the upper Oxus [River] valley" to require appointment of bishops.[15] In about 650 A.D. Jesu-Jabus speaks of Merv as having a "'falling church' because of a slow but steady defection of the Faithful to Islam." But still, "in 850 we find the line of metropolitans still continuing in ... Merv."[16] And there is evidence that about 893 A.D. there was a Metropolitan See based in Seistan.[17]

"Muhammad ibn-al-Qasim, advancing in 710 at the head of a considerable army, of which 6,000 were Syrians ... subdued Mukran, pushed on through what is now termed Baluchistan and in 711-12 reduced Sindh, the lower valley and delta of the Indus (Sindhu). Among the cities captured here were the seaport al Daybul, which had a statue of the Buddha (Ar. Budd) 'rising to a height of forty cubits,' and al Nirun (modern Hyderabad). The conquest was extended (713) as far north as Multan in southern Panjab, the seat of a renowned shrine of the Buddha where the invaders found a large crowd of pilgrims, whom they took captive."[18]

Presently, Buddhism is facing the grave possibility of extinction in its remaining two greatest strongholds: Myanmar (the ancient Burma) and Sri Lanka (previously known as Ceylon). The recent bestial expulsion by Buddhists of thousands of Muslims from Myanmar into East Pakistan seemed like a clear violation of the Buddhist doctrine "no harm to living beings." However, the Buddhists of Myanmar consider the expulsion of Muslims lawful in view of what Islam has done to Buddhism in the Indus River Valley in Pakistan and in the Bamiyan Valley in Afghanistan. With Islam's current attack against both Buddhists and Christians in Sri Lanka, Buddhists feel compelled to destroy Muslims rather than through indifference be destroyed by Muslims or become extinct.

§

---

1 Gordon H. Chapman, "Christianity Comes to Asia," The Church in Asia, Ed., Donald Hoke, (Chicago: Moody Press, 1975), pp. 182-183.

2 G. Le Strange, The Lands of the Eastern Caliphate: Mesopotamia, Persia, and Central Asia, from the Moslem Conquest to the Time of Timur, (Cambridge: The University Press, 1905), p. 487.

3 G. Le Strange, The Lands of the Eastern Caliphate: Mesopotamia, Persia, and Central Asia, from the Moslem Conquest to the Time of Timur, (Cambridge: The University Press, 1905), p. 338.

4 Dr. Wilson fails to point out that these crosses may rather be witness to a culture much older than Christianity. Dr. Byron L. Haines in "The Taxila Cross of the Lahore Cathedral," Al Mushir, Vol. XIII., Nos. 11-12 (Nov.-Dec. 1971), pp. 22-23 points out that equilateral crosses were ... in use throughout the

Chapter 1~Background: Christianity in the Center Arena

    whole history of Taxila." Further, "... a seal discovered at Mohanjodaro is engraved with a cross. Also, a very fine cross made of shell was discovered at Harappa. The last possible dating for either of these crosses is 1800 B.C."

5 J. Christy Wilson, Jr., Afghanistan, The Forbidden Harvest, (Elgin: David C. Cook Publishing Co., 1981) p. 68.

6 Gordon H. Chapman, "Christianity Comes to Asia," The Church in Asia, Ed., Donald Hoke, (Chicago: Moody Press, 1975), p. 182.

7 Unless it is the passage in the writings of Philostratus where he records the visit of Apollonius to Taxila.

8 Sir John Marshall, A Guide to Taxila, (Cambridge University Press, 1960), p. 27.

9 The poet R.T.H. Griffith more boldly portrayed the influence of the message of the suffering-savior, in his great panegyrical poem in praise of an unnamed king of Kasi, the name of an ancient kingdom in the region of present-day Banaras or Varanasi.

10 A.L. Basham, The Wonder That Was India a Survey of the Culture of the Indian Sub-Continent Before the Coming of the Muslims, (London: Sidgwick and Jackson, 1954), p. 276.

11 Ibn Hawqal "Flourished c. 943-977. ... He left Bagdad and began his travels in 943. He met al-Istakhri probably c. 952 and at the latter's request revised the maps and text of his geography. He then rewrote it and republished it under his own name, with the title 'Book of Roads and Provinces.'" – George Sarton, Introduction to the History of Sciences. (2 Vols.; Carnegie Institute of Washington, 1927-1931), Vol. 1, p. 674.

12 C.R. Beasley, The Dawn of Modern Geography, (3 Vols. London: Vols. 1 & 2, 1897-1901, Oxford: Vol. 3, 1906), Vol. 1, p. 454.

13 G. Le Strange, The Lands of the Eastern Caliphate; Mesopotamia, Persia, and Central Asia, from the Moslem Conquest to the Time of Timur, (Cambridge: The University Press, 1905), p. 408.

14 Kenneth Scott Latourette, A History of the Expansion of Christianity, Vol. 2: The Thousand Years of Uncertainity, (Grand Rapids: Zondervan Publishing House, 1976), p. 273.

15 C.R. Beasley, The Dawn of Modern Geography, (3 Vols. London: Vols. 1 & 2, 1897-1901, Oxford: Vol. 3, 1906), Vol. 1, p. 212-213.

16 C.R. Beasley, The Dawn of Modern Geography, (3 Vols. London: Vols. 1 & 2, 1897-1901, Oxford: Vol. 3, 1906), Vol. 1, pp. 219-220.

17 C.R. Beasley, The Dawn of Modern Geography, (3 Vols. London: Vols. 1 & 2, 1897-1901, Oxford: Vol. 3, 1906), Vol. 1, p. 242.

18 Philip K. Hitti, History of the Arabs, (London: Macmillan, 1968), pp. 210-212.

Heartland of the Middle East

CHAPTER 2

THE SETTING: AFGHANISTAN

Note: Be sure to see the corresponding map(s) in the Atlas Section.

As you will see, the first four Homeward-Bound Letters were written about our travels in Afghanistan. Perhaps some justification may be appropriate for devoting such a large portion of the letters to such a small land-locked country. My defense is, Afghanistan has had and continues to have an importance which belies its size as well as its land-locked location. Knowledge of its early Christian international outreach begins with an archaeological expedition in western China, right where Communist China is currently, with attempted secrecy, imprisoning thousands of Uyghur Muslims.

One evening, shortly before a spark ignited the Balkans and began a conflict which drew nearly all nations into the vortex of World War I, a group of German scholars and archaeologists were relaxing around a campfire after a day spent exploring the desert ruins of Turfan in far western China. The day had been rewarding because, among other things, they had retrieved an ancient book written in the Syriac script. However, the discovery was also frustrating because, though the book had been written using the Syriac orthographic system which they knew well,[1] that script had been used to transcribe a language which none of them understood.

Because of an 1899 scientific report by two Russian scholars, those German specialists had been drawn to the sand-covered ruins of the ancient caravan town of Turfan, which is now in far western China's Sinkiang Province.[2] Through that report it had become known that this site had been a major Buddhist center for many years and that rich archaeological treasures lay buried beneath its sands. Because of that information, several German expeditions, between 1902 and 1914, had extensively explored those ruins. Their investigations had focused on a part of the area then often called Chinese Turkestan. The ruins of Turfan are situated about 90 miles southeast of Urumchi (capital of present-day Sinkiang Province) at the foot of the Tien Shan Mountain range. That ancient city had flourished because it was an important junction on one of the major branches of the fabled Silk Road, a main artery of commerce between China, the Middle East and Europe, far to the west.

"North Asia's greatest cultural and intellectual communities evolved at the crossroads of intersecting caravan trails. At Turfan, Dunhuang, Kashgar, and other cities, travelers exchanged ideas and religious creeds along with their merchandise. Despite frequent raids by nomads, many of these oasis communities prospered for centuries as centers of artistic and intellectual achievement."[3] Scholars knew that among those who participated in the caravan trade on this artery of commerce between China and the West had been a people known as the Sogdians. "Through their mercantile activities [they], were the earliest Iranians to be in prolonged contact with China."[4] The language of the Sogdians "was the pre-Islamic lingua franca of Central Asia, with its center in Samarkand. It was replaced by Turkish languages in the New Iranian period [i.e., from the ninth century A.D. to the present]."[5] "The oldest form of the name of the country [the oases of Bukhara, Samarkand and probably part of the rich Ferghana Valley and other neighboring areas], in the old Persian inscriptions, is Sugd."[6] However, up to the time the German archaeological team was relaxing around its campfire, no one in modern times had been able to decipher Sogdian, that once common language!

That evening, as one German scholar casually but carefully turned those ancient pages, suddenly a name leapt up at him, recognizable because it had been spelled normally in a known alphabet. It was a name from the genealogy of Jesus as recorded in the Gospel of Matthew. At that moment the German scholars knew they had the key to understanding Sogdian, after many years' efforts during which no one had been able to unlock its secrets.

What had been retrieved was not Matthew's Gospel, but "some leaves and parts of leaves of a Gospel Lectionary[7] written, using Syriac letters, in the Sogdian language, a dialect of Middle-Persian."[8] Thus, that lectionary became a kind of Rosetta Stone, facilitating understanding of the Sogdian language once again.[9] Beyond the linguistic interest the discovery aroused, that lectionary also provides a testimony to the strength of the Christian thrust into China and Central Asia from the church in Sassanian Iran. It is also certainly possible that the Iranian church had begun that gospel outreach during the days of the earlier Parthian Empire which had been supplanted in 226 A.D. by the Sassanian Empire. Those early Christian evangelists not only had taken the message of Jesus to Central Asia and the Far East, they had also translated the scriptures into the language of those people! The existence of that lectionary indicates the presence of a congregation of Christians who used it in their worship!

For many years, Afghanistan served as the staging area and center from which Buddhist missionaries, following the trade routes, carried the message of Nirvana to China and also to the west as far as Rome. Homeward-Bound Letters Numbers 2 & 3 briefly discuss that amazing phenomenon.

As earlier in the case of Buddhism, Afghanistan later became a springboard from which the Gospel of Christ penetrated deep into China. As already noted, part of the evidence which leads to this understanding comes from the study of the rediscovery of the Sogdian language. The recovery of a Sogdian Gospel lectionary from sand-covered ruins in the Tarim Desert, in far western China, made it possible to unlock the mysteries of that once widely used Central Asian language. Beyond the linguistic interest that discovery arouses, it is a testimony to the

Chapter 2~The Setting: Afghanistan

strength of the Christian thrust into China which not only came through, but also came from an area that is now in Afghanistan. Thus, in a language of northern Afghanistan, which had died out by the Islamic period, the message of Jesus had been taken to western China!

The first Christian missionary known to have gone to China was Alopen. He arrived in the capital in 635 A.D. He probably not only came through what is now northern Afghanistan, but could well have been helped on his way by communities of Christians in that area. In a Chinese Imperial edict Alopen was called a "Persian monk."[10]

It should be remembered that Afghanistan, in turn, had been part of both Parthian and Sassanian Persia. The anonymous tenth century Persian geography, <u>Hudud al-Alam</u> [The title means "The Boundaries of the World."] clearly puts Herat in the Persian province of Khorasan. It says that Herat's "Cathedral mosque is the most frequented in all Khorasan."[11] The situation was well-summarized by Le Strange. He wrote, "Khorasan, as a province of medieval Persia, may conveniently be held to have extended only as far as the Oxus [River] on the northeast, but it still included all the highlands beyond Herat, in what is now the northwestern part of Afghanistan."[12]

That this early thrust of Christianity did come, in part at least, from Christians and Christian congregations in the area we now call Afghanistan is also confirmed by the discovery in 1625 in Hsianfu, China of the monument often called the Nestorian Monument. It had been erected in 781 A.D. near the capital city Ch'angan, as it was then known. "The stone was erected to commemorate the munificence of a Christian who had come from Balkh [The ruins of that once magnificent city are in present-day Afghanistan.] in the ancient Bactria in the vicinity of the Oxus [River], had risen to high favor in the Chinese government, and had been generous in the use of his wealth in caring for the poor and in restoring and enlarging monasteries <u>and churches</u>."[13]

As Afghanistan had been the base for an important expansion of Buddhism and Christianity, so it became the heartland and the power base of the Ghaznavid Empire (named for Ghazni, its capital city), the largest Muslim empire after the disintegration of the Abbasid Caliphate. (See Homeward-Bound Letter No. 4). At its apogee the Ghaznavid Empire stretched "from Iraq and the Caspian Sea to the river Ganges, and from the Aral Sea and Transoxiana to the Indian Ocean, Sind and the Rajputana Desert. Its greatest length from east to west was about 2,000 miles and its greatest width from north to south about 1,400 miles."[14] Thus, at that time, Afghanistan served as the staging area for the major expansion of Islam into India. Mahmud, ruler of the Ghaznavid Empire, "was the first sovereign to give practical shape to the idea of a Muslim empire in India."[15]

Heartland of the Middle East

A country which has generated movements of such scope, importance and impact cannot be dismissed as insignificant because some of its more superficial statistics, such as size and population, may currently not be particularly impressive.

On Christmas Day 1979, the Soviet Union invaded and partially occupied Afghanistan. That tragedy, which overwhelmed this strategic country, after Jonathan and I had partially explored its rich history, was an extension of a whole succession of tragedies.

What fascination brought Russia south in that astounding series of occupations? Mrs. Thatcher has given us one very penetrating analysis. She said, "The Soviets had long considered Afghanistan to have a special strategic significance and sought to exercise influence there through so-called 'Treaties of Friendship.' It was said that they were probably concerned, in the light of events in Iran, at the possibility of anarchy in Afghanistan leading to a second fundamentalist Muslim state on their borders, which might destabilize their own subject Muslim population. The West had for some time been anxious that the Soviets would make a drive for the oil in the Gulf. And the energy crisis gave them a still stronger reason to do so."[16]

These British artillery barrels, cast in 1798, now lying along a street in Kabul, were used in the first Afghan war which began in 1839. Though cast in 1798 they were still up-to-date weapons, giving powerful testimony of the determined upward thrust of an equally powerful empire, denying Russia of its desire to push through Afghanistan to British India and on to the Indian Ocean.

Note the date of manufacture for these artillery barrels (1798) and the representation of the royal crown of Great Britain.

Also, the desire to expand trade has undoubtedly been one of Russia's main motivations. But Russia realizes that to maximize the profit from trade, one must control its sources as well as its routes and terminals. However, each successive occupation of territory has also expanded Russian horizons and intensified Russian greed. How far will that greed entice the Soviets? How far can they go? Did the occupation of

Chapter 2~The Setting: Afghanistan

Afghanistan finally satiate Russia? The best answer to such questions may have been given in 1950 in a highly prescient analysis of Tsarist Russia by Fraser-Tytler who wrote, "There was in Central Asia no natural or man-made boundary on which the frontiers of Imperial Russia could rest. In the nineteenth century only one thing could stop this great southern expansion before it reached the Hindu Kush or even the shores of the Indian Ocean—the upward thrust of some equally powerful empire, challenging and arresting the mighty steamroller of Russia."[17]

It is hardly necessary to call attention to the obvious facts that Russia has already breached the wall of the Hindu Kush Mountains and that today there is no "upward thrust of some equally powerful empire, challenging and arresting the mighty steamroller of Russia." It seems altogether likely, then, that in the future we may see Russia pushing its occupation to the waters of the Indian Ocean. With Russia's expanded naval power those waters will probably not serve as a "natural boundary" but a means for further domination. What kind of timetable might we expect? One additional brief passage from Fraser-Tytler seems to set the parameters. He wrote, "After a pause to digest Samarqand and consolidate their acquisitions by establishing the province of Turkestan, General Kaufmann found himself embroiled with Khiva, where after a brief conflict the Khan was reduced to vassalage in 1873. To Sher Ali the omens were unmistakable, there was now only Merv and the Oxus [River] left between him and the Russians, and at any moment an influx of refugees might embroil him with his great neighbor in the north."[18]

The appropriateness of those omens pointing to the then current situation is obvious. The Soviets were beginning to digest Afghanistan and consolidate their acquisition. The "influx of refugees" put both Pakistan and Iran in grave danger of being embroiled with their "great neighbor to the north."

How Pakistan and Iran might easily have become even more deeply embroiled with the Soviet Union because of the refugee problem became clear from a news dispatch in *The New York Times* of January 1, 1983: "The Tass statement said that it was not the Soviet Union but 'imperialist powers, above all the United States of America and some other states,' that were responsible for the war because it was they who recruited 'bandit formations,' armed and trained them and then dispatched them into Afghanistan on missions of terror and subversion. Most Afghan guerrillas operate from rear bases in Pakistan and Iran."

How did Afghanistan manage to make itself so vulnerable to the Russian invasion? Why was it not anticipated? Why were Afghan forces not deployed on the northern border to check the Russian invasion at the border crossings on the Amu River? (The Amu was previously known by its Greek name, the Oxus River.) Why didn't Afghan army sappers blow up the Salang Tunnel (see paragraph four of Homeward-Bound Letter No. 1) if the northern perimeter could not be held? Why wasn't there a delaying action all the way to Kabul? Because there was a fifth column within the country which precluded any of these reasonable actions. But what gave opportunity for the rise of a fifth column in the country?

Here there is space only for reference to some of the main developments.[19] At the close of World War II Great Britain was forced, mainly by economic exhaustion, to forfeit its empire. The emergence of Pakistan and India, in what was formerly British India, left a great power vacuum in the region that presented the Soviet Union with an unprecedented opportunity to extend its influence south of the (Oxus) Amu River.

The United States, the only power then capable of filling the vacuum created by Britain's withdrawal from the Indian Subcontinent, declined the role. Its refusal was based on the assumption that American military assistance to Afghanistan would, in the first place, antagonize Russia. In the second place, American strategists thought military aid to Afghanistan would alienate Pakistan because of the Pashtunistan issue. At that time, Pakistan was considered by America to be the logical buffer in the region against Communist expansion and, therefore, should receive major military aid. Afghanistan advocated independence for the Pathan or Pashtun people. Success for the "Pashtunistan" scheme, which might have been insured by American military assistance to Kabul, would have taken many square miles of fertile territory from Pakistan.

Surprisingly, Mohammad Daoud, the president of Afghanistan at the time of the Communist coup, seemed not to have realized how detrimental his advocacy of Pashtunistan was, either while he had been prime minister or later during his presidency. For, "President Mohammad Daoud, a strong supporter of the Pashtunistan claim during his prime ministership (1953-1963), singled out Pakistan as the only country with which Afghanistan had a major political dispute, and declared his regime's full support for the right of the people of Pashtunistan for 'self-determination.'"[20]

America's refusal to grant military aid to Afghanistan drove Kabul to seek that aid from the Soviet Union. In that development, Mohammad Daoud was the pivotal figure, first as prime minister under King Zahir Shah and then, after seizing power on July 17, 1973, as president. Especially during his term as president he sought the support of Afghan Marxists to consolidate and enhance his own power. However, Daoud knew the danger of that policy and resorted to it during his presidency, only after another rebuff from America about a supply of arms.

Only ten days before Mohammad Daoud and his government officials were killed, I was in Kabul (on my way home from a visit to Pakistan) talking to a well-informed Afghan friend about these issues. My friend's recitation of events reminded me of the situation shortly before the first Anglo-Afghan war when King Ameer Dost Muhammad plead for support against Russia from the British through their representative, Burnes. Frustrated by the British indifference, Dost Muhammad reluctantly opened talks with the Russians. Similarly, after Daoud

Chapter 2~The Setting: Afghanistan

came to power he, according to my friend, appealed three times through the U.S. Ambassador for American military assistance. When no satisfactory response developed, Daoud, like Dost Muhammad years earlier, turned reluctantly to the Russians and even further toward the local Marxists.

Driven to seek their help, Daoud felt he was adroit enough to exploit the Marxists without giving them opportunity to build a power base. Recent history proves how tragically mistaken Mohammad Daoud was. He was overthrown and killed in a coup led by the Marxist Nur Muhammad Taraki in April 1978. The Taraki coup set the stage for the betrayal of Afghanistan into the hands of the Soviet Union.

As Afghanistan has served as a base for the advancement of Buddhism, Christianity, and, currently, Islam, so now it may also ultimately serve as a base for the advance of Communist militarism and imperialism.[21] The doors for Gospel outreach by the usual evangelistic methods have closed more tightly. Those areas bordering Afghanistan, which have been relatively open, are becoming far more difficult areas in which to work in the face of more and more stringent Islam and as Communism, especially working through China, sows chaos, tension, and insurrection as a step toward gaining control of those countries.

§

---

1 "The Syriac characters as used by the Nestorians gave rise to many Central Asian and Far Eastern alphabets such as the Mongolian, the Manchu, and the Sogdian. The existing characters of the two former groups of languages are lineal descendants of the original Uighurian forms which were certainly derived from the Nestorian Syriac characters, under the influence of the civilized Christian community of Uiguria." – A. Mingana, *The Early Spread of Christianity in Central Asia and The Far East; A New Document*, Bulletin of The John Rylands Library, (Nendeln, Liechtenstein: Kraus Reprint Limited, 1967), Volume 9, 1925, p. 338.

    Alphonse Mingana, while Assistant Keeper of Manuscripts in the John Rylands Library, was a special lecturer in Arabic in the University of Manchester. Three-quarters of a century after his research into the history of Central Asia, scholars are still richly rewarded by his work.

2 See Samuel N.C. Lieu, Manichaeism in Central Asia and China, (Boston: Brill, 1998), p. 3.

3 George E. Stuart, (ed.), *North Asia From 8000 B.C. to A.D. 1500, The Restless Frontier*, Peoples and Places of the Past, The National Geographic Illustrated Cultural Atlas of the Ancient World, (Washington, D.C.: The National Geographic Society, 1983), p. 277.

4 C.E. Bosworth, The Medieval History of Iran, Afghanistan and Central Asia, (London: Variorum Reprints, 1977), Chapter XIX, p. 12. "Sogdiana, ancient name for a region of Central Asia centering on the fertile valley of the Zeravshan, in the modern Uzbek Soviet Socialist Republic [now Uzbekistan]. Excavations have shown that Sogdiana was probably settled between 1000 and 500 BC and that it then passed under Achaemenian rule. It was later attacked by Alexander the Great and may have been included in the Bactrian Greek kingdom until the invasions of Saka and Yueh-chih peoples in the 2nd century BC. Sogdiana remained a prosperous center until the Mongol invasions. Under the Samanid dynasty (9th-10th centuries AD) it was an eastern focal point of Islamic civilization." – The New Encyclopaedia Britannica, 15th Edition, Micropedia, Vol. IX, p. 324.

5 Richard N. Frye, *Pahlavi Rule*, Colliers Encyclopedia, Vol. 13, 1971, p. 237.

6 Richard N. Frye, The Heritage of Persia, (Cleveland: The World Publishing Company, 1963), p. 43.

7 The word lection derives from Latin, meaning a reading. Thus a lectionary is "a book or list of lections to be read at church services during the year." The American Heritage Dictionary of The English Language, Third Edition. The fragments and leaves of that lectionary "contain sixteen quotations from Matthew, nineteen from Luke, fifteen from John, three from I Corinthians, and one from Galatians, and all are in almost complete agreement with the sacred text used by the Nestorian Church." – A. Mingana, *The Early Spread of Christianity in Central Asia and The Far East; A New Document*, Bulletin of The John Rylands Library, (Nendeln, Liechtenstein: Kraus Reprint Limited, 1967), Volume 9, 1925, p. 338.

8   F. C. Burkitt, The Religion of the Manichees, (Cambridge: At The University Press, 1925), p. 119. Surprisingly, a tiny group still speak a derivative of Sogdian. "The East Iranian dialects and languages, superseded by Farsi, have remained only in the most remote regions of the western Pamirs, in the territory of the present Gorno-Badakhshan Autonomous Republic (as part of Tajikistan): Yazgulami, Shugni, Ishkashimi, Roshani, and some others, constituting the Pamiri group of the East Iranian languages, and Yagnobi (in the Yagnob valley of Zeravshan), descending from the Sogdian language (with only 2,500 people speaking that language today)." – Vitaly V. Naumkin, Central Asia and Transcaucasia, (Westport, Connecticut: Greenwood Press, 1994), pp. 11-12.

9   The first time I learned of the thrilling account of the Turfan Christian scripture portions and the exciting implications for both linguistics and for understanding of the spread of the message of Jesus was at the University of Pennsylvania in 1958 during the lectures of the late professor Dr. Mark J. Dresden, an outstanding scholar of Persian history and culture and a specialist in the Sogdian language.

10 William G. Young, Patriarch, Shah and Caliph, (Rawalpindi: Christian Study Center, 1974), p. 172.

11 Hudud al-Alam, 'The Regions of the World,' a Persian geography 372 A.H. - 982 A.D. Translated by V. Minorsky. (London: Luzac & Co., 1937), pp. 103-104.

12 G. Le Strange, The Lands of the Eastern Caliphate; Mesopotamia, Persia, and Central Asia, from the Moslem Conquest to the Time of Timur, (Cambridge: The University Press, 1905), p. 382.

13 Kenneth Scott Latourette, A History of the Expansion of Christianity, Vol. 2: The Thousand Years of Uncertainty (Grand Rapids: Zondervan Publishing House, 1976), pp. 277-278.

14 Muhammad Nazim, The Life and Times of Sultan Mahmud of Ghazna (Lahor: Khalil & Co., 1973), p.169.

15 Muhammad Nazim, The Life and Times of Sultan Mahmud of Ghazna (Lahor: Khalil & Co., 1973), p. xiii.

16 Margaret Thatcher, The Downing Street Years, (New York: Harper Collins Publisher, Inc, 1993), p. 87.

17 W.K. Fraser-Tytler, Afghanistan: A Study of Political Developments in Central and Southern Asia. (London: Oxford University Press, 1967), p. 129.

18 W.K. Fraser-Tytler, Afghanistan: A Study of Political Developments in Central and Southern Asia. (London: Oxford University Press, 1967), p. 134.

19 Those wanting a comprehensive answer to this question should read the excellent exposition given by Nancy Peabody Newell and Richard S. Newell in their book, The Struggle for Afghanistan (Cornell University Press, 1981).

20 Amin Saikal, The Rise and Fall of the Shah (Princeton: Princeton University Press, 1980), p. 172.

21 Retired American Admiral, Elmo R. Zumalt, Jr., gives us a valuable, though very dated, appraisal. He said, "The Soviet invasion of Afghanistan also was the first phase of an ultimate thrust toward the Indian Ocean which would then swing both west and east. Soviet forces move 500 miles closer to the Indian Ocean, thus extending the encirclement of Middle East oil. Soviet bases in Syria, Iraq, Ethiopia, Mozambique and South Yemen already had contributed to that objective. Soviet-invading forces also moved across Afghanistan to the Pakistan border.

"The presence of these forces has made Moscow's subversive operations more effective inside Pakistan. When Moscow brings a Marxist puppet to power there, the Kremlin will have its long-coveted warm-water port from which to swing west to close the ring around Arabian and Iranian oil. (Chaos in Iran may bring that country's oil under Moscow's control earlier)."

"Soviet control of Pakistan bases will permit forces to swing east as well, thereby bringing pressure against India to shift from pro-Soviet neutrality to submissive cooperation with Moscow." – Elmo R. Zumwalt, Jr. and Worth H. Bagley, "A Soviet Southern Strategy?," The Journal of Commerce and Commercial, August 8, 1980, p. 4.

Chapter 3

The Silk Road

Homeward-Bound Letter No. 1
Kunduz, Afghanistan
October 15, 1975

Dear Friends,

Freya Stark aptly said, "Geography is behind trade, and trade is behind history."[1] She failed to remind her readers of an even more fundamental and important fact behind history. Thankfully, Daniel rendered that service when he wrote, "… the Most High ruleth in the kingdom of men."[2] So, God is behind geography, which is behind trade, which is behind history. However, we do not see this as pure determinism in history. Not only has God allowed us humans great freedom, but geography and trade also offer many options. Thus, within broad limits, man is still master of his own destiny.

Salang Pass Tunnel: The north-south one-way traffic takes turns being controlled by signal lights. ~ Michal Vogt - [1], CC BY-SA 2.0, https://commons.wikimedia.org/w/index.php?curid=7335181

On this trip we are trying to understand how men have used and are using their options.[3] Previous trips have always been by air and about the only evaluation we could make regarded the comfort, or lack of it, a certain aircraft offered, or the quality of service a given airline provided to economy-class passengers. This time we are driving through western Asia and have an opportunity to visit the arena of some of the most significant history of all time.

This morning, October 15, we are in a very frugal room of the Spinzar Hotel in Kunduz,[4] northern Afghanistan where we spent the night. To get here we traveled over the modern two-lane highway from Kabul which follows the route of one of the most important north-south branches of the ancient China-to-Rome Silk Road.

From Kabul to Kunduz, following a northern branch of the Ghorband River, we climbed into the heart of the great Hindu Kush Mountain Range. The name

"Hindu Kush" means "Hindu Killer." At the 11,600 foot elevation, the road enters the world's [then] highest road tunnel. This is the Salang Pass. Without the aid of this one-and-seven-tenths-mile-long tunnel, the silk, spice, and gem caravans of ancient times toiled hundreds of feet higher on the old trail, still visible, snaking up the steep talus slope. Even with the tunnel, the mountain pass is a real test for any vehicle as heavily loaded as our Jeep is.

The trajectory of the Hindu Kush Mountain tunnel helps one visualize the higher-up treacherous mountain trail used by men and beasts before the tunnel was completed. The roof-like structure above the tunnel is intended to deflect any falling stones from penetrating the tunnel structure. ~ By Scott L. Sorensen / mawg64 - My personal work, CC BY 3.0, https://commons.wikimedia.org/w/index.php?curid=14799602

As in ancient times, the major part of modern travel on this route is commercial. Content of the ancient trade may be visualized vividly from a glance at a stock list of the bazaar in Herat, one of the important transshipment points west of the Hindu Kush. Though this list applies to the time of Tamerlane (1336-1405 A.D.) and his son Shah Rukh (1377-1447 A.D.) it will give an accurate picture of much earlier times as well. "He (Tamerlane) took from its bazaars and caravanserais a treasure of 'silver, uncut gems, brocades and gold thrones,' all imported items. This was naught compared to the exotic items listed by contemporaries of Shah Rukh and Sultan Husain-i-Baiqara: damascened swords, bows inset with jade and tourmaline, drinking cups of Arabian coral, illuminated books and silks from the city itself, Bokhara rugs valued at ten diamonds each, unbored pearls and golden images from India. Fruit stalls offered such delicacies as Kabul's famed wild rhubarb, bananas from Ispahan and oranges from far Damascus." [5 & 6]

Chapter 3~The Silk Road: Letter No. 1

Though this photo shows the Amu River bridge with no traffic, as many as 400 cargo trucks travel over it every day between Afghanistan and Tajikistan. Tajikistan was part of Russia until the collapse of the Soviet Union. ~ *Photographer unknown: image from USACE via Wikimedia Commons.*

Today, trucks piled with manufactured goods from Europe and Russia, which they have picked up at the important Amu river port of Sher Khan Bandar (formerly known as Qizil Qala) along with indigenous items from northern Afghanistan (cotton, rugs, coal and cement), toil over the Hindu Kush to Kabul. Correspondingly, trucks heaped with export items from the south (fresh grapes, melons, fruits, skins and cereal grains) strain going north. On this route the most popular truck is International Harvester, followed by Bedford (made in England by General Motors). Then come various Russian models, followed by Mercedes Benz. In ancient times, of course, all trade was carried by man and beasts of burden, principally the camel, the ass and the horse. The yak, as king among beasts of burden, as it has been for centuries, still fills its role in extremely high, cold, and wet areas as in the Pamir Mountains in upper Badakshan Province.

Yesterday afternoon Jonathan and I drove north from Kunduz to within sight of the Amu Darya River. (Since the word 'darya' means river we should just say Amu River. However, there are many similar inconsistencies in other geographical names.) This is the Oxus River of the ancient Greek geographers.[7] It flows into the Aral Sea.[8] In addition to being the boundary between Afghanistan and Russia, it carries important water transport. We were turned back at the toll barrier just outside Sher Khan Bandar, the river port. To proceed further we needed special permission from the Police Commandant in Kunduz. In any case, the area is closed at sundown, which was imminent when we arrived. The port is a modern Russian contribution, as is the Salang Tunnel. Both have obvious strategic as well as commercial importance.[9]

Trade routes have played important roles in the spread of all major religions. Before Mohammad-bin Qasim subjugated the lower Indus Valley to Islam by the sword in 712 A.D., traders had already introduced Islam. Syrian Christian traders were important in making Christ known in Kerala on the southwest coast of India. Similarly, the Silk Road was a key factor in the spread of Buddhism. Trade provided two important elements for evangelism: contact and financial viability. Thus, "it was through Central-Asian kingdoms along the Silk Road that the Chinese first came in contact with Buddhism."[10]

The stimulus for the silk trade came from the wealth and opulence of Rome, where ostentation and extravagance increased with prosperity. Pliny, in his *Natural History* as quoted by the Latimores in their captivating book, describes the vast amount of labor involved in acquiring silk fabrics and then says, "So has toil to be multiplied; so have the ends of the earth to be traversed: and all that a Roman dame may exhibit her charms in transparent gauze."[11] (Doesn't that help us understand the relevance of 1 Peter 3:1-6?) Mrs. Nancy Hatch Dupree in her appealingly written and well researched book, A Historical Guide to Afghanistan, points out that silk "sold for $800,000 a pound in the Sybaritic markets of Rome."[12] (No, I didn't inadvertently hit an extra cipher or two when I typed that. She wrote, eight-hundred-thousand dollars per pound!)

The Alexandrian Greek monk, Cosmas, writing between 535 and 550 A.D., explained that the land route from China was a great shortcut for shipment of silk compared to the sea route. Thus it was preferred. He says, "loads of silk passing through the hands of different nations in succession by land reach Persia in a comparatively short time, whilst the distance from Persia by sea is vastly greater."[13]

On the way from Kabul to Kunduz we traveled very close to Kapisa (also known as Begram), the ancient summer capital of the Kushan Empire. The winter capital was Peshawar, now in Pakistan. In the Kabul Museum priceless treasures taken from Kapisa testify eloquently and convincingly of the wealth of the Kushans.[14] The area through which we have traveled on the Silk Road could have maintained only a very moderate population, as it does today, and perhaps it could have had a modest export of agricultural products. It certainly never could have sustained a magnificent empire like the Kushan. That was possible only because they exploited their situation as a major middleman in the silk trade. You may understandably wonder what brought it all to such a calamitous end, leaving only marvelous treasures of art and architecture to adorn museums. Two monks in the time of the Roman Emperor Justinian (b. 483, d. 565 A.D.) smuggled the eggs of the silk worm from India to Byzantium, and slowly an indigenous silk industry was established in the west which killed trade over the Silk Road.[15] The Chinese and Indians failed to protect their trade secrets well enough and great dislocation and suffering followed.

Not only did that technological breakthrough in the West suddenly erode the economic base of many Central Asian kingdoms, it led to their physical destruction. "They were less able to pay for peace and protection along the line of trade, and for this reason the nomadic tribes began to look to them for plunder instead of

Chapter 3~The Silk Road: Letter No. 1

subsidy."[16] This process eventually culminated in the total destruction brought by Genghis Khan that left most of Afghanistan in desolation from which large areas have not even yet recovered. The same process is graphically described by the Swedish traveler and writer, Jan Myrdal. Explaining the decay of the once great city of Maimana in northwest Afghanistan (we will not be able to visit that area) he remarks, "With poverty and the decay of trade comes banditry.[17] The nomads turn to plunder. With no caravans left for them to lead, the caravan drivers become roving robbers. ... In the oasis of Maimana, agriculture shrinks steadily. When no one any longer dares go there for fear of being attacked, the outlying fields have to be abandoned. ... The final act. The end of trade and industry. Of that proud merchant city nothing now remained. Of its civic culture, hardly so much as a memory. A filthy little village of clay huts among the sand dunes. The state of its peasants was indescribable. A few centuries had sufficed for a whole culture to be wiped out."[18]

The usual current methods of spreading the Gospel of Christ have become more and more difficult because of the proliferation of hypernationalism following World War II, to mention just one important reason among many.[19] In such a context, wouldn't an emphasis on evangelism through trade be in harmony with history and the present situation? James rebuked Christian traders in the Apostolic Age (James 4:13-17) but only because they forgot the ultimate goal of it all, the Lord's will (vs. 15).

May the Lord raise up devout Christian traders and businessmen in our day who will see their work not as an end in itself, but as a means through which the message of Christ can have new impact in areas where other means are extremely difficult or impossible!

Yours in Him who is the way,
Lee and Jonathan

---

1   Freya Stark, <u>The Minaret of Djam</u> (London: John Murray, 1970), p. 90.

2   Daniel 4:32

3   The more one reads history, especially Central Asian history, the more he is impressed that trade is a great determinant in human affairs. For example, W.K. Fraser-Tytler tells us that, "In 1842 the Russian frontier was still beyond the Sea of Aral, but as we have seen, the impulse to forestall the British in Central Asian markets and at the same time to protect Russian trade led to the first step in the great forward movement which in the next thirty years was to carry their influence to the Oxus." W.K. Fraser-Tytler, <u>Afghanistan: A Study of Political Developments in Central and Southern Asia</u>, (London: Oxford University Press, 1967), p. 127.

4   The centrality and significance of Kunduz was unmistakably underlined on October 8, 2021 when a mosque was bombed, killing scores of Muslim women gathered for the main Friday prayers. "The suicide bomber was a member of the Uyghur Muslim community, Islamic State says. ... At least 46 people were killed in the suicide blast. City health officials put the death toll at well over 100. ... A doctor at a Kunduz hospital run by the Doctors Without Borders aid organization said that, in his clinic alone, some 20 bodies were sent to the morgue and dozens of others among the 200 patients admitted were in critical condition. ... The floor of each intensive care unit is filled with blood—it's like a blood river." ~ *Dozens Killed in Afghan Mosque Blast*, <u>The Wall Street Journal</u>, October 9-10, 2021, p. A8.

5   Nancy Hatch Wolfe, <u>Herat a Pictorial Guide</u> (Kabul: Education Press, 1966), p. 62.

6   Amr ibn Bahr of Basra (d. 864 or 869 A.D.) gives a resume of the produce which poured into Baghdad from all over Iran. Iran in those days included what is now Afghanistan. The list from a much earlier time

makes an interesting comparison with the one from the days of Tamerlane. "From the land of Khwarizm: musk, ermine, marten, miniver, and fox furs; and very sweet sugar cane. From Samarkand: paper. From Balkh and its region: sweet grapes and Ghawshana truffles. From Bushanj: candied capers. From Merv: zither players, valuable zithers, carpets, and Merv suits. From Gurgan: grapes of various sorts, pheasants, excellent pomegranate grains, cloaks of soft wool, excellent raw silk. From Amid: brocaded suits, scarfs, fine curtains, and woolen veils for the head. From Damawand: arrowheads. From Rayy: prunes, mercury, woolen cloaks, weapons, fine suits, combs, 'royal' bonnets, *qussiyat* linen cloth, and pomegranates. From Ispahan: refined and raw honey, quinces, China pears, apples, salt, saffron, soda, white-lead, antimony sulphide, beds of several decks, extra fine suits, and fruit syrups. From Qumis: axes, saddle felts, parasols, and woolen veils for the head. From Kirman: indigo and cumin. From Ghur: cuirasses and psyllium. From Barda: fast mules. From Nisibin: lead. From Fars: *tawwazi* and *saburi* linen suits, rose water, water-lily ointment, jasmine ointment, and syrups. From Pasa: pistachios, various sorts of fruit, rare fruit, and glass ware. ... From Ahwaz and the surrounding region: sugar and silk brocades...castanets, dancing girls...extract of grapes, various sorts of dates, and sugar candy. From Sus: citrons, violet ointment, basil, horsecloth, and packsaddles. From Mosul: curtains, striped cloth, francolins, and quail. ... From Armenia and Azerbaijan: felts ... packsaddles, carpets, fine dates, cordons for drawers, and wool." – R.S. Lopez and I.W. Raymond, ed. & trans. Medieval Trade in the Mediterranean World. (New York: Columbia University Press, 1955), pp. 28-29.

7   A later reading note gives additional detail: "Below the Arhan ford the Oxus received the great right bank affluent, namely the Wakhshab or Wakhsh river, from which the Greeks, as already said, took their name Oxus; ... The Wakhshab is the river now known as the Surkhab, or Red River." – G. Le Strange, The Lands of the Eastern Caliphate; Mesopotamia, Persia, and Central Asia, from the Moslem Conquest to the Time of Timur (Cambridge: The University Press, 1905), pp. 435-436.

8   Essentially, the Aral Sea no longer exists. Russia diverted the water from the Amu (often still referred to by the Greek name Oxus.) and the Syr Rivers for the cultivation of cotton, depriving the Aral Sea of its means of rejuvenation. Today it is just a large puddle of muddy water. Large fishing boats that once plied its waters are now sitting on dry mud, being vandalized for usable parts. As the Amu flowed into the south end of the Aral Sea, so the Syr River flowed into the north end of the Aral Sea.

9   The strategic importance of the port and the tunnel was obvious when we tried to visit them in 1975. Just four years later the Russian's main route of invasion utilized these very facilities.

10   Owen & Eleanor Latimore, Silks, Spices, and Empire, (New York: Dell Publishing Co., Inc.,1968), p. 25.

11   Owen & Eleanor Latimore, Silks, Spices, and Empire, (New York: Dell Publishing Co., Inc.,1968), p. 12.

12   Nancy Hatch Dupree, An Historical Guide to Afghanistan, (Kabul: Afghan Tourist Organization 1971), p. 26. Also, how the spice trade stimulated the economy may be understood if we realized that, "Before the first Europeans dropped anchor in Asia, they could obtain spices only at exorbitant prices and from Arabs who brought them overland. Pepper was worth its weight in gold. In England during Middle Ages cloves served as currency. In Germany, a pound of nutmeg could buy seven oxen. The spice trade supplied much of the wealth that helped bring about the Italian Renaissance. For centuries spices were a significant force in the global economy." – Clayton Jones, World Monitor, July 1990, p. 59.

13   Owen & Eleanor Latimore, Silks, Spices, and Empire, (New York: Dell Publishing Co., Inc.,1968), p. 18.

14   For those interested, see Nancy Hatch Dupree, Louis Dupree, and A.A. Motamedi, The National Museum of Afghanistan An Illustrated Guide, (Kabul: The Afghan Air Authority and The Afghan Tourist Organization, 1974).

15   A later, more detailed, reading note may interest many of you: "We are told by Procopius in his Gothic War of certain monks who told Justinian that while it was impossible to transport silk worms or moths from China, eggs could be brought. By generous promises he persuaded them to do this. According to a fragment from another historian preserved by Photins, they kept them warm in dung concealed in their staffs, and at the beginning of spring put the eggs on the mulberry trees that formed their food, and the worms feeding upon these leaves developed into winged insects and performed their other operations." – George Every, Understanding Eastern Christianity, (London: SCM Press Ltd., 1978), pp. 25-26.

   Also, "The establishment of this industry was another of the triumphs of Justinian. All silk had previously been imported from the East, but during his reign some eggs were smuggled into the Byzantine Empire and soon the silk worm flourished on mulberry trees by the Bosporos; in later generations the rich and patterned textiles were a feature of the court and much-prized presents to the west.

16   Owen & Eleanor Latimore, Silks, Spices, and Empire, (New York: Dell Publishing Co., Inc.,1968), p. 11.

17   As a confirmation of Myrdal's observation that, "With poverty and the decay of trade comes banditry," compare the observation of Ibn Butlan about conditions in Ressafa in the eleventh century in footnote 1,

Chapter 3~The Silk Road: Letter No. 1

Homeward-Bound Letter No. 11.
18 Jan Myrdal and Gun Kessle, <u>Gates to Asia</u>, trans. Paul Britten Austin, (New York: Pantheon Books, 1971), pp. 56-57. Since the time so graphically described by Myrdal, Maimana has experienced a great economic revival.
19 It is easy to sympathize with the feelings behind much hyper nationalism. After all, the people in many of the countries which came into existence at the end of World War II had been forcibly merged into western imperial creations.

Heartland of the Middle East

Chapter 4

The Giant Buddhas

Homeward-Bound Letter No. 2
Bamiyan, Afghanistan
October 21, 1975

Dear Friends,

For three days Jonathan and I have been exploring one of the world's most unusual and significant valleys. The word "valley" may suggest a low elevation but the floor of this one is 8,480 feet above sea level! To get here one has a choice of three mountain passes: the Unai-Hajigak Pass at 10,665 feet [the one we used], the Shibar Pass at 10,501 feet or the Salang Pass, which we mentioned in our first letter, at 11,600 feet. Only the last one has a paved road. The first one, though not the highest, is clearly the most difficult. The walls of the valley and the surrounding mountains which tower above it are nearly as colorful as the painted desert. Here, in the Bamiyan Valley, one is far from industrial pollution and the full beauty of this exquisite place with its sparkling cold mountain stream and its dazzling display of stars at night delivers an indelible impact. As delightful as these

A panoramic view of the Bamiyan Valley showing the two perpendicular excavated recesses which housed the gargantuan images of the standing Buddha.

natural beauties are, they did not call us here. In this valley are magnificent as well as frighteningly condemning monuments of human history. Carved in the north wall of the valley are two statues of the standing Buddha. The first one has been standing for seventeen hundred years and the other for sixteen hundred years. These colossal monumental Buddha statues are in the very heart of the Hindu Kush Mountains of Afghanistan.

As formidable as the route through these mountains is, it has always been less arduous to endure the cold and snow of this route than the much more severe winter cold and snow of Russia if one wished to go from China to Rome or vice versa. Also, by this route one avoided the barbarians of central Europe who would only have plundered the caravans. Besides, Persia was the transshipment point of the eastern part of the trade. From Persia everything would be sent on to Rome. To get to Persia from China or India, people had to go through one or the other branches of the "Silk Road" which traversed Afghanistan. The Bamiyan Valley was one of the favorite routes between the Far East and Persia.

During the early period of its empire, Rome was rich and growing. At the same time the Han Dynasty was brilliantly ruling China. India, with its exotic wealth, also invited trade. Therefore, the Silk Road throbbed with commerce between these three great centers. The Kushan Empire, astride this great trade route (ruling from Bactria to the Ganges River), was enriched by the opulent trade which came through its territory. The Kushan's third and greatest king, Kanishka, who ruled ca. 130 A.D., recognized Buddhism, though by no means exclusively, and gave it state patronage. His coins honored a whole pantheon of deities. Kanishka, like the Roman emperors far to the west, accepted deification.

Kanishka called a great Buddhist council in Kashmir which revitalized Buddhist philosophy by recognizing the Mahayan concept. This state patronage and enlarged concept finally found expression at Bamiyan in the third century A.D. by the sculpturing of the smaller of the two colossal Buddha figures, and

This altar was probably part of the great temple at Surkh Kotal. It may have been the place where King Kanishka was granted deification, and, from that ceremony, was recognized as the leading figure in Mahayana Buddhism.

Chapter 4~The Giant Buddhas: Letter No. 2

in the fourth century A.D. by the sculpturing of the larger one which is technically superior.

These, the world's most extraordinary and spectacular images of Buddha, tried to express the cosmic significance of Buddha and his message, as conceived by his devotees. The new expanded message of Mahayana Buddhism was developed by adapting concepts from the Gospel of Christ which had reached Afghanistan and northwest India early in the Christian era. (See page 10.) However, to discuss that cross-fertilization at this moment would take attention away from Bamiyan.

In the Bamiyan Valley, carved in the side of a perpendicular cliff, were the world's two largest statues of the standing Buddha. Those gigantic statues were there until the year 2000 when, despite a worldwide outcry, the Taliban destroyed them with artillery fire. The shorter statue was 115 feet tall, equal to the height of a modern 12 story building. The larger statue was 174 feet tall, equal to a modern 18 story building. When were those marvels crafted out of the sheer cliff? We know they were there fourteen centuries ago when the Chinese Buddhist monk Hsüan-tsang beheld them in 630 AD as he came through Bamiyan on his pilgrimage to Buddhist sites in India.

Heartland of the Middle East

To sculpt the two gigantic Buddhas and the maze of interconnecting passageways in the cliffs around them, and to plaster and ornament the huge excavations in the cliff in which they stand must have been an epic challenge to some of the greatest engineers, craftsmen and artisans of the world at that time. Buddhist monks by the thousands thronged the valley. Today, their cells, meeting rooms, and chapels still honeycomb the cliff for about two miles in Bamiyan Valley. Buddhist missionaries from this great center, following the trade routes, carried the Buddhist concept to China and to the west, at least as far as Rome.

Bamiyan, "at its height … was filled with life and activity, covered with galleries, staircases and balconies, brilliant with stucco brightly painted in the designs and iconography of Greece and Rome, Persia, China and India, reds, blues, green, yellow, white, orange, gold, flanked by the two great niches where the standing images … glowing with color, towered two hundred feet over men like Hsüan-tsang who, in 632, had walked (!) hundreds of miles to come to this Valley of the Gods and center of Buddhist faith."[1]

"In order to envision this view as it was during the days of its greatest splendor one must imagine the facades of all the caves painted in rich polychromatic hues enhanced by sculptured figures, also painted. The colossal figures were coloured and glistening with ornaments, the smaller in blue, the larger in red, faces and hands gilded. In addition, there were stupas and buildings all along the base of the cliff, such as the king's monastery mentioned by Hsüan-tsang which was certainly gayly bedecked with banners and canopies as depicted in the wall paintings of Kakrak."[2]

Today there are no monks here. The visitors, both transient and resident, who perambulate around the Buddhas do not do so in adoration, as did Hsüan-tsang and other Buddhist devotees, but do so out of awed curiosity. No prayer flags snap in the breeze and no missionaries are sent out from this valley to spread the Buddhist message of Nirvana. To understand why, remember that 632 A.D., the year Hsüan-tsang (the Chinese monk) visited Bamiyan on a pilgrimage, was also the year Mohammad died. By the time he died, Islam was triumphant in the entire Arabian Peninsula. Only nine years later, in 641, Arab armies in the name of Islam conquered the Sassanian Empire in Persia. In only another 58 years, in 699, the Arabs had pushed their conquest to Qandahar in southeast Afghanistan. But it was the Muslim Turks, under Soboktagin, working out of their base at Ghazni, about 970 A.D., who conquered the Buddhist king of Bamiyan and brought Buddhism in this valley to a violent end. Buddhism is by principle, and has often been in practice, pacifist. It is a mark of the ethical decline of Buddhism that near its close here they maintained an army and engaged Soboktagin's forces in battle. This outward catastrophe was a reflection of an inner disaster.

Muslim kings ruled from Bamiyan from the time of Soboktagin till an even greater disaster overwhelmed this lovely valley. In the interim, the Muslims defaced the giant statues and desecrated every wall painting they could reach in

Chapter 4~The Giant Buddhas: Letter No. 2

their zeal to destroy idols. In 1222 A.D. a Muslim king, Sultan Jalal-Din Manguberti, was ruling Bamiyan. In that year, the Mongol, Genghis Khan, came south conquering and to conquer. The city of Bamiyan was well-defended by outlying fortresses at the approaches to the valley and by a mighty inner citadel. After overwhelming the formidable outer fortresses, today still standing in ruins, Genghis Khan penetrated to the heart of the city and besieged the citadel.

The citadel was built on a large, extremely steep hill which was crowned by enormous battlements and towers. Inside the walls were cavernous underground cisterns to supply water during a siege. These were fed by an elaborate system of tunnels. Against the eventuality of an attack, grain was stored in warehouses roofed with brick domes. At the pinnacle of the bastion was the ultimate defensive position, a high fort with every conceivable defense. It is a frightening testimony to the cruel military genius of Genghis Khan that the entire citadel today lies in ruins and is called the City of Weeping because of the helpless and pitiful final cries of its doomed inhabitants and defenders.

The Red City, one of the outer defenses of the valley, as we beheld it.

Every living thing was killed in that holocaust. Genghis wrought such havoc and destruction in the valley, destroying even the intricate irrigation system, that areas still lie in arid desolation that once were lush farm lands. After 753 years the evidence of destruction is still shocking. A mighty fortress city, splendidly adorned by brilliant ceramic art, enjoying the wealth of this once fabulous trade route, lies in awesome ruins. Truly, they (whether they be Buddhist, Muslim, or Christian) who take the sword shall perish by the sword! (Matthew 26:52)

Heartland of the Middle East

The most widely accepted tradition explaining Genghis Khan's ruthlessness says, thinking the defenses of the valley insignificant, he had sent his grandson as leader of a small force to take it. The defenders fought fiercely and killed the young Mongol in their zeal. In reprisal for the death of his grandson, Genghis Khan vowed to kill every living thing. A more reasonable explanation is found in a Muslim historian's account, <u>Tarikh-e Tabari</u>, written about one hundred years after the Bamiyan holocaust. In that account it is asserted that the grandson was sent as a leader of a delegation seeking a peace treaty between the Mongols and the people of Bamiyan. The delegates, according to that account, were all beheaded and their heads sent back to Genghis Khan as an answer to his quest for peace!

Utter destruction of ancillary defenses protecting the main fortress.

This leads me to a bit of speculation in the "What if?" department. What if Buddhism had been loyal to its principle of pacifism till Soboktagin came? Would it have been permitted to survive under tight controls? Many diverse religious groups were allowed to continue in the onward rush of Islam. Had it survived, could it have converted Genghis Khan when he came? If not, could they at least have exercised an ameliorating influence and have saved untold thousands from violent death? Could they have saved incalculably valuable works of art, engineering, medicine and science from oblivion? Many years earlier, Buddhism had converted a great king and military leader, Ashoka of India who renounced war after his armies had killed some 100,000 in the battle of Kalinga, in eastern India. We shall never know because we are now speculating about how history might have been.

Chapter 4~The Giant Buddhas: Letter No. 2

One thing is certain. Because a religious community was disloyal to one of its highest ethical ideals, it never had the opportunity to save great areas from the scourge of the Mongols. Let us pray that we may walk worthily of our heavenly calling in Christ that we may be a means of blessing when the need and opportunity arise.

                        In the name of the Prince of Peace,
                        Lee and Jonathan

---

1   Richard Leavitt, "Bamian the Valley of the God's," Fodor's Islamic Asia, Iran – Afghanistan – Pakistan, Ed. Robert C. Fisher, Nina Nelson (New York: David McKay Co., 1974), p. 429.

2   Nancy Hatch Dupree, The Valley of Bamiyan (Kabul: Afghan Tourist Organization, 1967), pp. 23-24.

Heartland of the Middle East

Chapter 5

Alexandria of the East

Note: As you read Homeward-Bound Letter No. 3, you will realize afresh that the small border city of Qandahar has held a highly important position in local and international affairs from the time of the great Indian King Ashoka (who reigned 268–232 B.C.), to the present. It has been one of the key points of military power for the American forces assisting the Afghan army against attacks from the Taliban. The military significance of Qandahar was made vivid again in a news item in <u>The New York Times</u> dated 11/18/20: "Now, with President Trump's order to cut American forces in Afghanistan by roughly half—from 4,500 to 2,500—Kandahar's fate, and the fate of the Afghan security forces spread across the country are once more in question."[1]

Homeward-Bound Letter No. 3
Qandahar, Afghanistan
October 28, 1975

Dear Friends,

Today, October 28, Jonathan and I are in Qandahar in southeast Afghanistan. Here, during his lightning-like thrust to the east, Alexander the Great established one of the many cities in Asia which he named Alexandria in his own honor.[2] There may have been an earlier city on the site, but in any case, Alexander recognized the strategic importance of this place and left Greek colonists, administrators and troops to hold it for his new empire. This location controls the easiest access routes to Kabul and the Hindu Kush Mountains on the north and to India in the east. "Down through the ages caravans and armies have moved incessantly from Iran and Central Asia to India. On their way they encountered the mighty mountains of the Hindu Kush, a most formidable barrier. To avoid the rigors of its passage many wound their way around its western end and followed the skirts of the Hazarajat [homeland of the Hazara people] to their southern limit at Kandahar."[3]

The empire which Alexander so skillfully and dramatically carved from the old Persian Achaemenid Empire proved ephemeral. As Daniel prophesied, the he-goat (Greece) lost much of its stunning power when its "notable horn" (Alexander) was broken. (See Daniel 8:1-14.) After Alexander's death, most of the area became part of the patrimony of his general, Seleucus Nicator, founder of the Seleucid Empire. Its western capital was the new city of Antioch in Syria. Selucas and his three competitors for the spoils of Alexander's Empire were the four horns which sprang up after the one notable horn was broken. (See Daniel 8:8-9.)

Alexandria, present Qandahar, with its vast hinterland known to the Greek geographers as Arachosia, was ignobly ceded to the Mauryan Empire of India in exchange for just 500 elephants and one beautiful princess! So the city and the

Heartland of the Middle East

whole vast territory came under the rule of India's greatest Mauryan, Emperor Ashoka, who reigned 268-233 B.C.

Ashoka's Account

Https://commons.wikimedia.org/wiki/File:AsokaKandahar.jpg

1. Ten years (of his reign having been completed), King
2. Piodasses (Ashoka) made known (the doctrine of)
3. piety to men; and from this moment he has made
4. men more pious, and everything thrives throughout
5. the whole world. And the king abstains from (killing)
6. living beings, and other men and those who (are)
7. huntsmen and fishermen of the king have desisted
8. from hunting. And if some (were) intemperate, they
9. have ceased from their intemperance as was in their
10. power; and obedient to their father and mother and to
11. elders, in opposition to the past also in the future,
12. by so acting on every occasion, they will live better
13. and more happily (Trans. by G.P. Carratelli)

This Greek inscription, engraved by order of King Ashoka, who reigned from 268–232 BC, should help us understand the significance of the inspired statement by the apostle Paul to the Galatian Christians in which he wrote, "when the fulness of the time came, God sent forth his Son." (Galatians 4:4) Part of the 'fulness of time' was that moment in history when an adequately expressive language had become the vehicle of international communication. Obviously, Greek had become the most well-known international language as far east as Qandahar. However, we know its use had gone appreciably further east because of Gondophares, the Greek-speaking king, who reigned at Taxila. From the ruins of Taxila, gold coins minted by King Gondophares are inscribed in Greek. We do not know how much further east Greek had become a common language.

Certainly when the apostle Thomas (who brought the Gospel to Taxila, resulting in the conversion of King Gondophares) went to south India, he was completely out of the area in which any Indo-European language was spoken. At that point in his ministry, he undoubtedly relied upon linguistic ability which was given to him through the gift of tongues. (See I Corinthians 12:10-28.) Concurrently with the international use of Greek with which to convey the Gospel message, other factors also developed. Perhaps the most important one of those factors was the development of road systems, not only in the Roman Empire, but as far east as the Iranian government prevailed. Taxila, today, is a small town about 25 miles west of Rawalpindi, Pakistan.

During Ashoka's reign the most popular means of mass communication was by rock and monumental pillar inscriptions. This is reminiscent of the inscriptions of Darius I at Behistun, between Hamadan and Kermanshah in modern Iran and of the much more ephemeral wall posters of modern China. Ashoka used the medium often and his inscriptions and edicts have been discovered at many places in the Indian Sub-Continent. In his great series of surviving inscriptions, Ashoka usually urges all to embrace non-violence as a way of life, as he had when he embraced Buddhism. Of special interest to us are the two westernmost Ashokan

Chapter 5~Alexandria of the East: Letter No. 3

inscriptions so far discovered. Both are here in Qandahar. The first one to be discovered was written in both Greek and Aramaic, the language Jesus spoke. (Shown in photo at left.) The second inscription is longer and is entirely in Greek.

The inscription was placed at a conspicuous spot on the side of the road which led to the Middle East. It was this road on which Ashoka's Buddhist missionaries traveled, carrying Buddhism's message of *The Four Noble Truths* and *The Eight-Fold Noble Path* to the West. As we mentioned in our letter from the Bamiyan Valley, Buddhism was usually monastic. Professor Dupont-Sommer suggests that the monastic concept which was embodied by the Essenes may well have been presented to them by the Buddhist monk-missionaries on their westward preaching tours. So, Qandahar may hold the clue to the origin of the Essenes!

Reflecting on the great political, military, commercial and religious interactions between East and West, even during the third century before Christ, it is certainly clear there was a precedence and means for the evangelistic tour the apostle Thomas is alleged to have made to India. The ancient document, The Acts of Saint Thomas, provides one source of evidence that Thomas did, indeed, preach Christ in India. Keeping in mind the historical accuracy of the document's incidental details (for example, the mention of King Gondophares who was not known from any other source till his coins were recovered in large quantities when Taxila, now in Pakistan, was excavated) we realize it may well be an authentic document of apostolic history. However, the extant text had been tampered with by the Manichaeans who put their doctrines in the apostle Thomas' mouth when he preached!

We consider it a high privilege to have visited Qandahar even briefly. The present city has a frontier flavor. Indeed, it is a frontier city. It is the first major Afghan city or town one reaches if he enters Afghanistan through Quetta from Pakistan. That is why both Pakistan and India maintain consulates here. Many of the streets are unpaved and its many small single-story shops are closed by wooden shutters.

It is not only architecturally and commercially like a frontier town but, for the most part, we found it open and friendly. Quite contrary to that atmosphere was the presence of ridiculous petty officialdom. In Qandahar, Ahmad Shah Durani, the father of modern Afghanistan, is buried. We visited his tiled mausoleum and wanted to take pictures of some of the beautiful glazed tile arabesques and some of the very fine incised calligraphy on stone medallions set in the walls. The soldiers on guard forbade photography! We wondered, how can a grave be strategic? We went away disappointed.

Heartland of the Middle East

Ahmad Shah Durani's mausoleum

On a basalt mountain overlooking the city is a place where the Mongol kings inscribed their deeds. Though it has been a tourist attraction for centuries, access is now forbidden by soldiers! Also, the Ashokan inscriptions are on private land to which access is not given. So our visit could be classified as "sweet and sour." We hope we emphasized the sweet! Maybe it will be even sweeter next time, if God grants a next time. If not, we've tried to savor the present opportunity as fully as possible. Thank you, Lord!

All for now, coming your way,
In Christ,
Lee and Jonathan

---

1   Thomas Gibbons-Neff, Najim Rahim & Fatima Faizi, *American Troops are Packing Up, Ready or Not*, The New York Times, November 18, 2020, p. A1.

2   It is remarkable how similar the name Qandahar is to the name Alexandria. The phonetic similarity between the modern and ancient names is striking. The letter 'x' in the name Alexander corresponds to the 'Q' in Qandahar, which is sometimes spelled with the 'K' rather than the 'Q'. The three letters 'a-n-d' are identical in both 'Alexander' and 'Qandahar.' The differences between ' er' and 'ar,' the final two letters in the name, are simply two ways of expressing the same phonetic value.

3   Nancy Hatch Wolfe, Herat a Pictorial Guide (Kabul: Education Press, 1966), p. 58. Mrs. Wolfe in her statement "… to their southern limits …" refers to the Hindu Kush mountains, not to the Hazarajat, the home of the Hazara people.

Chapter 6

Slaves to Conquerors

>Homeward-Bound Letter No. 4
>Herat, Afghanistan
>November 2, 1975

Dear Friends,

In our last letter we commented on Qandahar. This time we'd like to make a few observations about Ghazni, Bost, and Herat which, as you will notice, leapfrog over Qandahar.

Ghazni is some eighty miles south of Kabul on the way to Qandahar. Today, Ghazni is a small city of general merchants and antique vendors clustered around the old mud fortress walls that were breached by the British in the first Afghan War (1838-1842). There are now army barracks located in the citadel area of the fort, which precluded the possibility of curious foreigners poking around.

Ruins of the Ghazni Fort

Ghazni is in a position to block the approach to Kabul from Qandahar. Because of its strategic position it has been repeatedly built and destroyed. It had been an important Buddhist center from the Kushan period to at least the eighth century A.D. An Italian archaeological team is doing a really splendid excavation of the old Buddhist center at a site in Ghazni called Tapa Sardar. They have uncovered a large reclining Buddha, badly damaged, and later Hindu deities in remarkably good condition, especially considering they were all molded from clay.

Ghazni was destined to become internationally important shortly after the Muslim Turkish slave, Alptigin, conquered the fort in 962 A.D. and founded the Ghaznavid Dynasty. (Obviously, named from Ghazni.) The greatest ruler of that dynasty was Sultan Mahmud, more widely known simply as Mahmud of Ghazni. He was a military genius and an ardent advocate of Islam. After expanding his power base by conquering Kabul, Bost, Balkh, Herat, and parts of Eastern Persia (all between 977 and 1000 A.D.) he began a series of seventeen iconoclastic military campaigns into India. Through these, Islam, in its Sunni form, spread in a major way in the Indian Subcontinent. From the plunder, Ghazni was enriched beyond calculation. The greatest architects, engineers, artists and literati were enticed to Ghazni to transform it into a dazzling capital for the new empire.

One of Mahmud's victory towers at Ghazni, his capital city which he built by loot. This tower also served as a minaret for the mosque.

To avoid the severe winter cold of Ghazni, the fortress of Bost at the confluence of the Arghandab and the Helmand Rivers (as the road now goes, a distance of 305 miles to the southwest of Ghazni) was selected as the winter capital. In addition to the court, Mahmud's 2,500 war elephants were taken there every winter to save them from the rigors of the cold in Ghazni. (The number varies from 1,700 to 2,500 elephants.) The ruins of the fortress at Bost testify to the accuracy of the contemporary accounts of its greatness as a center of trade and administration. Along the banks of the Helmand, the nobles and ministers of the Ghaznavids built winter villas whose regal-looking ruins still stretch for more than a mile. In the heyday of Ghazni, both the Arghandab and Helmand Rivers were thronged by silk-draped pleasure barges during the winter months. It was the

Chapter 6~Slaves to Conquerors: Letter No. 4

Ghaznavid Riviera. We found Bost the most temperate of all the places we visited in Afghanistan, but we suspect the heat would be almost penal in the summer.

The breathtaking glory of Ghazni was deliberately destroyed by two punitive military expeditions: first (ca. 1150 A.D.) by Alla-ud-din Ghori, who earned the epithet "The World Burner," and the second by Genghis Khan (ca. 1221 A.D.) which irremediably destroyed the city when it had just begun to recover. All that remains of that once glorious city are two truncated, but still elaborate, victory towers which were built in memory of Mahmud's military successes. Originally they also served as minarets for two imperial mosques. Today, the mosques are gone and the towers stand at the edge of a large cemetery! There can be no more eloquent testimony than Ghazni's, that "all flesh is grass, and all the goodliness thereof is as the flower of the field: the grass withereth, the flower fadeth; because the breath of the Jehovah bloweth upon it: surely the people is grass." (Isaiah 40:6-7 ASV)

Looking through the repairs of a victory arch on the way south from Ghazni. The buildings in the distance are ruins of Mahmud's winter retreat at Bost.

Many stories survive about the court of Mahmud. We particularly like one about Aiyaz, his chief minister who had been elevated from extremely humble circumstances to a position of awesome power. Much like Daniel's peers, the other ministers of Mahmud's court became jealous and looked for some way to bring him down. They noticed that each morning, in the privacy of his chamber, he opened a small box, peered in for a moment or two and then, with evident satisfaction, re-locked it. They reported these strange actions to Mahmud, suggesting that Aiyaz was probably gloating over loot stolen from the Crown. Summoned before Mahmud, in the presence of the cabinet, he was ordered to produce the box and open it before the king and his court. When the box was opened only a soiled, badly worn set of commoner's clothes was found.

Heartland of the Middle East

Asked to explain his strange habit of opening the box every morning with such obvious solemnity and satisfaction, Aiyaz told the court he only wanted to be sure that he never forgot what he was before the king had called him into his service, and how the king had elevated him. He wanted his sense of gratitude and humility to be renewed each morning. We think how worthy his attitude would be for every Christian. (Please read II Peter 1:9.)

Mahmud's "court was famed throughout the Middle East for its garland of more than four hundred poets, philosophers, artists and other learned men. Here shone such dazzling lights as <u>Al Biruni</u>, the astronomer-mathematician; <u>Firdausi</u>, the poet-historian; <u>Ansari</u>, the king among poets; <u>Hakim Sanai</u>, the Sufi philosopher, doctor and poet, and many, many others."[1] There is no space here to fully tell how Firdausi, under the promise of patronage from Mahmud, worked in poverty for some thirty years to complete the greatest epic poem of all time. Its sixty thousand captivating verses preserve the greatest myths and noblest history of Persia. Added to my original letter, here is a very short excerpt:

"High in the midst of the embattl'd host
Young Hoshung stood, the royal Persian's boast.
Onward each army rush'd with martial glow,
Revenge and empire dwell upon the blow.

Immortal vigour fir'd the Persian train,
And clouds of dust o'ershadow'd all the plain.
Proud and audacious! dauntful in the fight,
The demon rov'd, too confident of might.

His strokes on all re-echo, all engage,
As when the roaring lion hurls his rage.
The old king trembled, as he view'd the force
Of the dire demons mow their dreadful course;

'Twas then brave Hoshung with undaunted might
Sought the young demon thro' the thickest fight.
They met, they fought, the hero's patriot glow
Gave force and vigour o'er the treach'rous foe.

Long was the combat, when the prince's arm
Struck the pale demon, trembling with alarm.
Then hurl'd him from his courser, as he fled,
And as he fell, he lopp'd his impious head."[2]

Chapter 6~Slaves to Conquerors: Letter No. 4

Firdausi's dignified memorial at Tus, Iran, his hometown.

After his great work was presented to the king, the poet was not properly recompensed. In bitter disappointment, just before his premature death, he wrote a withering, cutting poetic satire of the king. While Firdausi was writing, the king repented and sent the promised bounty, which Firdausi had not wanted for himself but to finance an irrigation system for the people of his hometown of Tus, in northeastern Iran. Legend says that when the royal messengers, bearing the apologies of Mahmud and 60,000 gold dinars, one for each verse, as the king had himself suggested at the outset, entered "Tus by the Rudbar Gate, the body of Firdausi was being carried out to the cemetery by the Rizan Gate."[3] If you would like to read some of Firdausi's great poems in English, ask your local librarian for <u>The Epic of the Kings</u>, by Reuben Levy, published by Routledge in 1967.

And so from Ghazni via Qandahar to Bost and on to Herat. We arrived in Herat late on Thursday night, October 30 or, more precisely, very early on the morning of Friday, October 31. Our visas would expire November 2nd and we would have to cross the border by sundown on that day, at the latest. Just

before reaching Herat the armature in our generator burned out (after more than twenty years of faithful service) because a bushing had failed. So, precious time had to be devoted to repairs which deprived us of the kind of look at Herat it deserves. It was the Hairava of the Achaemenids, it was conquered by Alexander. It was the springboard of Islam in its push to the east. It had the most magnificent buildings in all of Asia, it

A very old minaret in Herat with a close-up of the beautiful turquoise blue faience work.

was a great center of commerce and culture and we had to spend most of our precious final hours getting the armature rewound!

The few settled communities through which the road passes are characterized by a unique type of windmill known as the Herat Windmill. These are built on top of the mill house, that is, the house where the millstones are located. The windmill is a structure on the roof, but has no resemblance whatsoever to the windmills of Holland or to those on western ranches in the United States. In the region of Herat the windmill shaft is made of a tree trunk about twenty-five feet long, like a telephone pole, which rests upon the top millstone and extends vertically through the roof of the mill house. Two circular walls built on top of the mill house at 180 degrees from each other carry a transverse beam with a bearing in the middle into which the top of the vertical shaft fits. From the vertical shaft radiate about six sets of equally spaced spokes. To these spokes vertical reed-mat sails are attached which, catching the incessant wind blowing across this steppe country, rotate the shaft, thus spinning the upper millstone.

Due to over-heating of the Jeep engine at this point, (the only occasion on which over-heating happened during our entire trip) I was unable to shoot my own photo. The Herat wind was blowing with such velocity and angle that the jeep engine fan, at this location, could not pull in enough air to keep the engine within its heat limits. ~ Photo: © Roland & Sabrina Michaud/akg-images

Chapter 6~Slaves to Conquerors: Letter No. 4

The circular support walls are so arranged that the sails are exposed to the wind in only one portion of their cycle and protected from the wind on the return portion of the cycle, so the reverse thrust of one sail doesn't cancel the forward thrust of another. The Arab geographers described these unique windmills as early as the seventh century A.D., which antedates the use of windmills in either Europe or China.

There is a west wind called the Herat Wind that is said to blow for 120 days, from June to September. Well, what we experienced was a north wind in November! In any case, Afghanistan could profitably do a study on the potential of wind power used for generation of electricity, with modern equipment, in the area contiguous to Herat, but especially between that city and the Iranian border in the steppe country. We suspect it has tremendous potential.

In addition to its glory there was also a dark side to Herat. It was a great slave market in ancient and medieval times. The favorite source of slaves was the mountainous region of Ghor to the east, where the people were non-Muslim and, therefore, fair game. Later, it was Turkish slaves. Slaves were often part of the booty of war. For example, Alexander sold 30,000 of the captives of ancient Tyre into slavery.[4]

We thank God that Christ fought a war to free us from slavery and now proclaims release to us captives (Luke 4:18-19).

Your fellow slaves in Christ,
Lee and Jonathan

---

1 Prita K. Shalizi, Here and There in Afghanistan, (Kabul: Education Press, 1966), p. 18.
2 Trans. J. Champion, Persian Poems, An Anthology of Verse Translations, ed. A. J. Arberry, (NY, NY: E.P. Dutton Inc. & Co., no date), p. 187.
3 Fredrick Tallberg, From Cyrus to Pahlavi A Picture Story of the Iranian Empire, 2nd ed. (Shiraz: Pahlavi University, 1967), p. 50.
4 Another glimpse of the size of the slave trade comes from the account of the return of Mahmud of Ghazni from his invasion of the Ganges Doab. He brought back 55,000 slaves taken captive in war. Cf. Mahammad Nazim, The Life and Times of Sultan Mahmud of Ghazna, (Lahore: Khalil & Co., 1973), p. 110. The Hindu Kush mountain range, as I mentioned in my first letter, means the Hindu Killer. "According to Ibn Bututa, [the range] has derived its present name from a dreadful role it was made to play in killing by the inclemencies of its terrain and weather the millions of Hindu prisoners dragged through its recesses by Muslim conquerors of the Middle Age." – N.D. Ahmad, The Survival of Afghanistan, (Lahore: People's Publishing House, 1973), p. 52.

Heartland of the Middle East

Chapter 7

Glimpses of Afghan Life

In Letter No. 5, I remark about the great progress in many areas of life in Iran compared to that which had been achieved in Afghanistan. In reviewing my letters for this book, I realized that I had not really emphasized current life in Afghanistan in a way that would make it possible for you to feel the same sense of development in Iran that we did when we crossed into Afghanistan's neighboring country to the west. For that reason, under eight categories, I have made this selection from our photos of life in Afghanistan. These photos will help you visualize normal life, with remarkable clarity, as we beheld and experienced it.

Bedouin Life: In addition to sedentary life in Afghanistan in its permanent villages and towns, there is a significant Bedouin population which migrates within the country as pasture for their flocks seasonally develops enough for grazing. These Afghan tribal people live in clusters of tents made of black goat hair. They are masters of moving with their possessions and flocks to re-establish temporary tent-based residence at locations which are able to provide adequate pasturage. This photo shows the encampment of a thriving tribe.

Heartland of the Middle East

Economic disparity is seen in the simplicity or sophistication of the tribal camps. The photo above shows the bleak circumstances of a poor tribe. The labor-intensive work of dismantling, packing, driving the animals, and erecting a new camp falls largely to the women. These pastoral tribes show their determination and expertise by constantly leading their flocks to new places to graze. The cows, goats and chickens provide basic food for the tent people.

Sedentary Population Pressure: Both within and beyond established city/town limits, one observes an explosive expansion of jerry-built houses which are occupied as soon as they can give shelter to desperate couples seeking stable conditions for themselves and their children. Notice in this photo that parents were so pressed to provide shelter for their growing family that doors and windows would have to come later, after occupation. Also, in steep clusters of houses like these on the hillside there are no roads or streets, only foot traffic is possible.

Glimpses of Afghan Life

Agriculture: Through many centuries, the wooden plow pulled by oxen has proven to have been a tremendous advance in agriculture. That fact becomes obvious when one compares ox-plow agriculture to that carried on in much more limited plots prepared for seeding by family members using only hand trowels or hoes.

The frame of the most primitive ox-plow is made entirely of wood. Fastened to the bottom on the leading edge of the vertical timber is a small iron cutter, technically known as the colter. It extends below the surface level of the soil and makes furrows for planting. Plowing by tractor in Afghanistan was so insignificant during the time of our visit that you could say it was nonexistent. Note the switch in the farmer's hand. If one ox slacks off, the furrow will be crooked.

The cornucopia of potatoes shown here testifies to the success of primitive agriculture carried on in Afghanistan's Bamiyan Valley. The soil is fertile. During the growing season the weather is benign. Unless some agricultural disaster, like the Irish potato famine occurs, basic food items will be adequate to carry the stable resident population through till the next harvest season. This is maintenance, not export agriculture.

The Cutting Edge: Sharpening knives and other cutting tools was a two person effort. One worker powered the grinding wheel while the other held the cutting tool at the proper angle to sharpen its blade. The gross inefficiency of this grinder is seen, first of all, in the necessity of two people to operate it. Also, when the belt has been pulled to its full length by using one hand, the rotation of the grind wheel will reverse as the other end of the belt is pulled!

The development of human powered grinders took a major step forward by the invention of a treadle powered grinding wheel commonly used on American farms before electric power became available. The improved model was both operated and powered by a single person sitting on a bicycle-type seat, turning the grind wheel in only one direction by the use of foot pedals.

Glimpses of Afghan Life

Country Dining: There are good restaurants in Kabul and in all the major towns, but in rural villages and bazaars only basic arrangements are available. Still, we found the food to be flavorful and nourishing. The main item on the menu was usually some variety of curry. It is served with naan with which one picks up morsels of his food. Notice the colorful, small porcelain tea pot just behind Jonathan's right hand. Simplicity doesn't need to exclude all elegance.

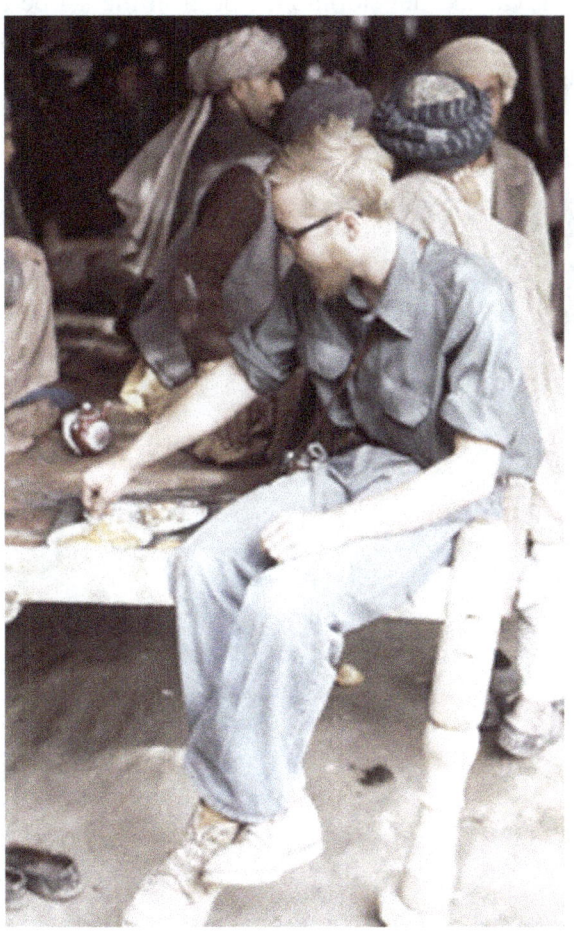

Domestic Utensil Repair: In villages, the repair of cooking and serving utensils takes place in tiny shops like this one. This makes it possible to offer an appreciable advance of services compared to the work of an itinerant tinker. These shops provide customers advanced developments, both in the scope and technical quality of their work. Not only is repair work carried on in shops like this but customers can hire them to put a metallic silver-looking surface on their copper utensils.

Glimpses of Afghan Life

Rural Shopping: Aside from agriculture, in rural towns and villages of Afghanistan, small bazaars are the center of economic activity. Here, Jonathan is surveying the scope of products being sold in this rural town bazaar. Everything needed to support individual and family activities is usually available. The shopkeepers specialize in the products they offer. Therefore, there is little overlap in their wares. Despite the specialization practiced by the shopkeepers, collectively, they offer everything needed to carry on ordinary life in rural and remote areas in Afghanistan.

Domestic Industry: If a family can spare a few square feet from its living space it can accommodate a small carpet loom. The threads of the warp are kept taut by gravitational energy which is generated by weights pulling a beam to which the threads of the warp are attached. The whole process, including assembly of the loom, twisting and dying the thread, following a beautiful design, can all take place in a villager's home. The sale of such domestically produced artistic carpets can compete well with those produced more mechanically. The return on a family's labor is an important compliment to its budget.

Chapter 8

The Setting: Iran

Obvious Significance

Here, in contrast to the discussion of "The Setting: Afghanistan," there is no need to raise the question, "Why Iran?" Painful memories of the American diplomatic staff being held hostage and of the atrocities of SAVAK (the Shah's secret police) are too fresh and too powerful for anyone even yet to doubt the timeliness of interest in Iran. The stunning irony of the incomparably more numerous and more vicious atrocities under Khomeini, on whom the nation bestowed power, partly in hope of deliverance from tyranny, forces all of us to take notice of Iran. The interminable Iran-Iraq 8-year war, with all its tragedy and potential for spreading further disaster, has pushed the vital importance of Iran before our notice every day. Now, Iran, siding with the dictator of Syria in his war against his own people, and Iran's all-out effort to produce atomic weapons, has put everyone on high alert.

Roots in a Great Historical Past

Much of the Arab world had no significant history before the rise of Islam. "The Arabs before the time of Mohammad had been a collection of rival tribes or clans, excelling in the savage virtues of bravery, hospitality and even chivalry, and devoted to the pursuit of booty."[1] Therefore, the Arab people feel Islam has given them their history. Iran, on the other hand, looks back to pre-Islamic times for its greatest period of glorious history. (This may be the very reason why Khomeini, at one point after coming to power, threatened to have the magnificent ruins of Persepolis totally destroyed! He didn't want such powerful testimony that Iran was great, long before Islam.)

The name Iran, derived from the name of the great Aryan people, reflects the ethnic origin of the nation. The name Persia, until quite recently the more familiar name, is the Greek form of the name Pars. Pars is the name of the province which was the political and administrative center of the country when Iran was at its peak of power, ruling over everything from the Aegean Sea in the west to the Indus River in the east, and from the Black Sea to the Indian Ocean, north to south. Those were the glory days when Iran's kings were truly emperors, "who reigned from India unto Ethiopia" in an empire so vast that for efficient administration it had to be divided into "a hundred and seven and twenty provinces."[2]

In those challenging times, military success, diplomatic virtuosity, and economic vitality produced an empire so secure it could follow an internal policy toward oppressed and displaced peoples which was gracious, indeed. It was a benign and humane policy which was in stark contrast with the policy of its predecessor, Babylon, which gathered "captives as the sand,"[3] and whose king, Nebuchadnezzar, slew whom he would, "and whom he would he kept alive; and whom he would he raised up, and whom he would he put down."[4]

Heartland of the Middle East

It was in such circumstances that "Jehovah stirred up the spirit of Cyrus king of Persia" to decree that the captive Jewish people should freely go "to Jerusalem, which is in Judah, and build the house of Jehovah, the God of Israel (he is God)."[5] The release of Jewish people from captivity was typical of the policy of Persia toward most captive people in their empire in those times. Even following the death of Khomeini, Iran is far more reminiscent of Babylon under Nebuchadnezzar than Iran under Darius the Great.

Beginnings of the Iranian Church

Long lines of chained,[6] mocked,[7] and sexually molested[8] Israeli captives were led to the area now known as Iran by the Assyrians and, later, by the Babylonians when they in turn exercised their cruel and tyrannical jurisdiction over the area. No one at that time could have imagined that one day from those pitiful captives' progeny would come the charter members of the Messiah's church in Iran, but that is certainly what happened. Except for any proselytes who may have been among them, those from Parthia, Media, and Elam who were present in that audience which heard the first declaration of the Gospel of Christ[9] were ethnically all Jews, all descendants of those captives, and were nationally all Iranians or Persians.

When those who had accepted Christ on that Day of Pentecost, and during those subsequent days of triumphant preaching in Jerusalem, returned to Iran, they constituted Christ's initial Iranian church. Those initial Iranian converts must have shared their new knowledge and their new faith with many of the diaspora who were their neighbors and with many "native" Iranians as well. In this way they would have added a new dimension to the fulfillment of Micah's prophecy that "the remnant of Jacob shall be in the midst of many people as dew from Jehovah, as showers upon the grass."[10]

In Iran, as well as in the Roman Empire, there was a people prepared to accept Christ, for many Iranians had become converts to Judaism.[11] They, along with the ethnic Jews in Iran, probably had some anticipation of the coming of the Messiah through study of the scripture.

The earliest surviving writing from any of the Persian Christians are the sermons of Aphraat who lived in the first half of the fourth century.[12] "His sermons stress the need for asceticism."[13] He also expressed "pro-Roman sympathies."[14] As pointed out in Letter No. 7, it was the latter sentiment rather than the former which got the Iranian Christians into serious trouble.

Unique Conditions for the Church in Iran

From its inception, the church in Iran, under the Parthians as well as under the Sassanians, faced a situation perceptively different from that which prevailed for the church in the Roman Empire. The church in both empires suffered imperial persecutions. Also, the church in both empires evangelized the heathen beyond their imperial borders. From Rome, missionaries pushed across the Rhine and

Chapter 8~The Setting: Iran

even crossed the English Channel to tell the heathen of Christ. Similarly, missionaries from Iran pushed into Central Asia (that is, Asia north of the Oxus River, [now called the Amu], and lying between the Caspian Sea and the Pamir Mountains). The Gospel was even taken beyond the Pamirs to China. Unfortunately, however, the church did not survive in Iran as it did in western Europe. Some causes may be identified which date from the beginning of the career of the Iranian church and even before.

To start with, the religious system of the Zoroastrian Iranians "had been constructed with much more art and solidity than the uncertain mythology of Greece and Rome."[15] Thus Iran, as a whole, never became congenial to the Gospel.

Another significant difference was the nominal Christian stance of the barbarians who invaded western Europe while the barbarians invading Iran at roughly the same period were totally hostile to the Gospel. Historically, Iran exercised liberality toward minority movements when it felt its economy was not threatened by doing so. In the Achaemenian period, Cyrus could be liberal and generous to captive people because the trade routes and their termini were securely in Iranian control. Thus, releasing the captives in no way endangered this pillar of Iranian prosperity. But Iran would show little mercy to citizens who embraced a teaching which seemed to ally them with myriads in the Roman Empire, which was their mortal economic and military rival.

The Shah and His Overthrow

The late Shah of Iran was indeed repressive. However, his record in that regard should not be assessed only by comparison with concepts of freedom in the U.S., but must be evaluated by comparison with the historic situation in Iran. Was it from that perspective an improvement or a regression? Also, the Shah's record should be assessed not only by comparison with the historic situation in Iran but with contemporaneous regimes in the Middle East. Such a comparison is flattering to the Shah, for "most Middle East rulers were cruel and by their standards he was a liberal."[16] Two powerful Iranian vested interests conspired to defeat the Shah: the secular feudal landlords and the religious feudal landlords, that is, the Mullahs (a Mullah is a learned teacher or expounder of the law of Islam). Any land reform which broke up the vast estates controlled by feudal landlords and feudal Muslim religious organizations in favor of private ownership by the land-tilling peasants would, inevitably, be hated and opposed.

The Mullahs could easily enlist the uninformed and unenlightened peasantry in violent protests under the banner of loyalty to Islam. Thus the peasantry sided with a system which would ensure the continuation of their own captivity in serfdom. It was largely analogous to the Marxists' enlisting the peasants of Russia under the cry of "the dictatorship of the proletariat" when, in fact, such dictatorship actually proved to be against the very proletariat by whose strength it had come to power!

The Shah attempted, as it were, to mix oil and water but never achieved a stable emulsion. He tried to blend the Iranian cultural heritage, Islamic theology, and Western democracy. From the Iranian cultural heritage he stressed, particularly, the idea of Macro-monarchy, that is, the emperor-king ("God-king" is closer to the historical reality), known in Iranian history as "king of kings." But, Islamic theology has its own inherent concepts of polity and economics. He failed to recognize, till far too late, that the mixture was incompatible. General Zia-ul-Haqq, president of Pakistan by a military coup, saw the reality of the situation far more perceptively when he said, "Pakistan's present political edifice is based on the secular democratic system of the West, which has no place in Islam. ... This country was created in the name of Islam and in Islam there is no provision for Western type elections."[17]

Obviously, one immediately wonders what part democracy would have in a society dominated by a monarch. The Shah spoke of "imperial democracy." He said, "The union of these two words should not be surprising. According to Iran's constitution, be it that of 1906 or 1950, although the Emperor submits his projects for acceptance by the government, he nevertheless remains a constitutional monarch. He reigns but does not rule."[18] Further, the Shah's answer was "that by 'political democracy' he meant the blend of the Western principle of parliamentary [system] with the Persian monarchial tradition!"[19]

The Shah apparently was committed to drastically altering the monarchy. He said, "Threatening developments [during the Allied occupation of Iran during World War II] could not easily scare me into abandoning the principles of such men as Thomas Jefferson, principles I was determined to follow."[20]

In harmony with his commitment to democracy, the Shah seemed to feel he should be an elected sovereign. However, his concept of election was far-fetched. He considered the enthusiastic popular support for the Monarchy at the close of Mossadegh's attempt to bring Iran under Communism an election! He wrote, "I returned to Tehran where I was greeted with popular enthusiasm. Throughout Iran the people were undeniably behind the crown. Before, I had been no more than a hereditary sovereign, but now I had truly been elected by the people."[21]

If one looked only at the evidences of prosperity visible everywhere in the country at the time Jonathan and I explored Iran, it would seem inconceivable that chaos, religious persecution, revolution, mob rule, and widespread killing could come so quickly as they did.

Several factors contributed to those cataclysmic events. Paramount was the continuing desire of the Soviet Union to implement the Czarist design by pushing to the warm waters of the Indian Ocean. The Czarist imperative was augmented by the powerful modern one: the desire to control the oil of the Middle East. Two events were crucial to destabilizing the entire area. First was Britain's withdrawal from the Indian Subcontinent in 1947, followed twenty-four years later by the

Chapter 8~The Setting: Iran

withdrawal of its fleet from the Persian Gulf as part of its wider withdrawal of all forces east of the Suez in 1971. Iran, under the Shah's leadership, tried valiantly but vainly to fill the void.

The United States' refusal to give military aid to Afghanistan because of the latter's espousal of Pashtunistan was the second crucial event which destabilized the area. It made Iran's eastern flank extremely vulnerable to Russian exploitation. The Shah could not provide for Afghanistan what the United States might have provided.

§

---

1 Stanley Lane-Poole, quoted by John Bagot Glubb, War in the Desert, (London: Hodder and Stoughton, 1960), p. 19.

The reason the Arab world was devoid of significant history before the rise of Islam may well be the concessions the Bedouin, in his tribal and disunited pre-Islamic period, had to make to his harsh environment: "He has conquered the desert by his ability to go without the comforts of life; little water, rare meat, no permanent home, the stony ground to lie on at night. His pleasure is to suffer, his satisfaction is to abstain, and this has left his soul bare and primitive: he has no sense of aesthetics, no refined sensibilities, no philosophy, literature, art, no complex mythology even, for all these adornments of the human spirit have been stripped off and cast aside by the Bedouin as useless encumbrances in the battle to survive." – Robert Lacey, The Kingdom (New York: Harcourt Brace Jovanovich Publishers, 1981), p. 29.

2 Esther 1:1 ARV
3 Habakkuk 1:9 ARV
4 Daniel 5:19 ARV
5 Ezra 1:1-3 ARV
6 Jeremiah 40:1 ARV
7 Psalm 137:3 ARV
8 Lamentations 5:11 ARV
9 Acts 2:9 ASV
10 Micah 5:7 ASV
11 Esther 8:9-17 ASV
12 Of course, earlier records are preserved in the works of later writers. For example, an account of Christianity in Iran from 99 A.D. through 541 A.D. called the Chronicle of Arbil was written by Mashihazakha between 541 and 569 A.D. Till 1974, the only translation was in French by Alphonse Mingana, Sources Syriaques Vol. 1, published in Leipzig in 1907.

For a most helpful evaluation and many informative extracts translated into English see William G. Young, Patriarch, Shah and Caliph, A Study of the Relationships of the Church of the East with the Sassanid Empire and the Early Caliphates up to 820 A.D. with Special Reference to Available Translated Syriac Sources (Christian Study Centre: Rawalpindi, 1974).

13 M.A. Smith, The Church Under Siege (Downers Grove, Illinois: Inter-Varsity Press, 1976), p. 88.
14 M.A. Smith, The Church Under Siege (Downers Grove, Illinois: Inter-Varsity Press, 1976), p. 88.
15 Edward Gibbon, Christianity and the Decline of Rome, (New York:: Collier Books, 1962), p. 139.
16 Paul Johnson, Modern Times The World From the Twenties to the Eighties, (New York: Harper & Row Publishers, 1983), p. 704.
17 *Islam Takes Over*, Asia Week, November 2, 1979, p. 16.
18 Mohammad Reza Pahlavi, Answer to History, (New York: Stein and Day Publishers, 1980), p. 129.
19 Amin Saikal, The Rise and Fall of the Shah, (Princeton: Princeton University Press, 1980), p. 80.
20 Mohammad Reza Shah Pahlavi, Mission For My Country, (London: Hutchinson & Co. Publishers, Ltd., 1974), p. 77.
21 Mohammad Reza Shah Pahlavi, Mission For My Country, (London: Hutchinson & Co. Publishers, Ltd., 1974), pp. 90-91.

Heartland of the Middle East

CHAPTER 9

THE THRESHOLD OF ASIAN MODERNITY

>Homeward-Bound Letter No. 5
>Mashhad, Iran
>November 5, 1975

Dear Friends,

Today, November 5th, we are in Mashhad, Iran. It is spitting snow so we plan to stay here, holed up in our room at the state-run campground, till the weather becomes more cordial.

We crossed the border into Iran about sunset on November 2nd. That had required the two most rigorous border inspections we have ever experienced. Traffic in marijuana, of course, is from India, Pakistan, and Afghanistan toward the West.[1] Coming into Afghanistan from Pakistan there was no examination of baggage whatsoever, but to keep narcotics from flowing west, the examination at Islam Qala, the Afghan Border Post west of Herat, is minute. Every bag goes on a table and is opened and examined. Side panels, floors and ceilings of the vehicle are carefully scrutinized. There is an under-the-hood examination and the vehicle is examined underneath from a pit. The principle upon which the operation was carried out seemed to be, "You are guilty until proven innocent."

A few kilometers later, at the Iranian Border Post, the same procedure took place, only with greater politeness, finesse and thoroughness. When both scrutinies were finished it was well after dark. We were tired and decided to find accommodation in Tayebad, the first town in Iran, only 22 kilometers from the border check post. Early the next morning we drove the 224 kilometers on to Mashhad, our present location. We are happy to have an economical spot to catch up with letters, laundry, servicing the Jeep, and other essentials.

From Herat, Afghanistan to the Iranian border is steppe country. There are a few mud brick villages, but the most impressive habitations are the large clusters of black goat-hair tents of the nomads.

They tend large herds of camels and flocks of sheep on an "open range" basis. One has to be careful lest his rig be totaled out by a romping camel! (See also Chapter 7, Glimpses of Afghan Life.)

Heartland of the Middle East

Once across the border, change becomes immediately noticeable. First is the modernity of the border control center on the Iranian side. It has, as far as we could ascertain, every facility that the U.S. or Canadian control points would have at Blaine, Washington, for instance. All that modernity, with cafeteria, tiled restrooms, modern offices and soldiers in impeccable uniforms, stands in marked contrast to the ramshackle facilities on the Afghan side. Leaving the border control area, we were immediately impressed by the much higher standard of highway engineering compared with Pakistan and Afghanistan. The basic paved roads in Afghanistan are good because, for the most part, they have been engineered and built under the auspices of the Russian or American foreign aid programs, but refinements are absent. There are no white lines, no reflecting highway signs, and very few distance markers. All these are present on Iranian roads. Driving is easier and more pleasant. Of course, there is much more traffic, which counterbalances the benefits to some extent.

This line of trucks hauling sugar beets to the factory demonstrates that farming in Iran had reached an industrial scale. During peaks of harvest season, the processing mills run around the clock. Still, trucks have to wait to be unloaded.

Another notable impact on coming into Iran is what I call big-sky farming. We saw only two areas in Afghanistan in which farming compares with what we have seen in this eastern part of Iran's Khorasan Province: Afghanistan's Helmand Irrigation Project around Bost, and some dry-land farming between Samangan and Khulm. Here, in Khorasan, sugar beets are being cultivated on a large scale. Big truck-and-trailer outfits are out in the fields loading, to carry the crops to the mills. Wheat fields extend as far as one can see. Tractors haven't completely replaced animal-powered farming but they are nearly everywhere.

The towns along the highway are obviously sharing the benefits of Iran's increased Gross National Product. Big silver-painted municipal water towers rise above the towns. The highway through the towns is usually divided with a well-

Chapter 9~The Threshold of Asian Modernity: Letter No. 5

cared-for parkway in the center and is well-lighted by mercury vapor highway lamps. All this is possible because of increasing national income since the discovery of oil in May 1908 at Masjid-e-Soleyman, and the enlightened and benevolent monarchy of the Pahlavi dynasty that finally achieved stability after the ouster of the recalcitrant Prime Minister, Dr. Muhammad Musaddiq, in August 1953.

This beet sugar factory is working at full capacity, but even so, cannot accept the harvest quickly enough to keep the trucks from long delays.

Mashhad is one of the great emotional and devotional centers of the Shi'ite branch of Islam, the national religion of Iran. Here, the eighth Imam, or Leader, is buried. The mausoleum is the most beautiful and most venerated in all Iran. Including tourists as well as devotees, some four million people a year throng this religious center.

Shi'ism is obviously flourishing, but what about the religion of Christ in this great city of 750,000, the third largest in Iran? A brief note in *The Bulletin of the Fellowship of Faith for Muslims for June, 1975* is graphic: "Mashhad, a city of pilgrimage for many Shi-ite Muslims in Iran, is situated near the Afghan border.

Five years ago this place had a thriving church of over 100 members, then the hospital closed and the missionaries left.[2]Today there is no pastor, and only a handful of people. Do please pray." We have had dinner twice with our friend, Dr. Howard Harper, Chairman of the Department of Ophthalmology, University of Mashhad. He is sent out by the New Zealand Brethren Churches. He fully confirms the statement in *The Bulletin*. The work which was closed was Presbyterian.

Heartland of the Middle East

Apparently there is no Christian group in this entire city, except a small one meeting in the Harper home. Pray that Christ may have an effective witness in this great city.

> With prayer to the Lord
> of the Harvest,
> Lee and Jonathan

A mausoleum in Masshad. Shi'ism is obviously flourishing, but what about the religion of Christ in this city of 750,000 (the population when we visited)?

---

1 It is appropriate to add, as a later comment, that Khorasan had, until the late Shah's very serious crackdown on the trade, a thriving business in opium from its extensive fields of poppies. How serious the Iranian government's efforts were to stop the traffic in drugs was emphasized by displays of contraband narcotics in the show cases in the custom service's buildings. Also on exhibition were the traveler's luggage and clothing in which the contraband had been concealed.

2 Evaluating this, subsequent to the overthrow of the Shah: Can something of practical value be learned from this experience about how Christ's great commission (Matthew 28:18-20) should be carried out, at least in Muslim areas? H. B. Dehqani-Tafti, Iranian Bishop of the Episcopal Church in Iran, which has been severely persecuted since the Khomeini revolution, gives an evaluation of the institutional missions of which the hospital in Mashhad was a part, which should be carefully considered. Regarding the earlier trouble experienced by the Episcopal Church during the crisis when Prime Minister Mussadeq nationalized the Anglo-Iranian Oil Company (the expropriation law was approved by the Majlis on April 19, 1951), Bishop Dehqani-Tafti wrote, "Looking back nearly thirty years, it is easy to say that we ought to have read the writing on the wall and accommodated ourselves to the spirit which brought about the oil crisis. Instead, it seemed to us to be God's will that the hospital should remain in the hands of the church. I am sure now that the right thing would have been somehow to have 'nationalized' our hospitals and indeed our other institutions. The American Presbyterians, who perhaps saw better the signs of the times, closed, handed over, or sold all their seven hospitals in the north of the country. We were reluctant to close down good and useful establishments, but we would have been wise to negotiate with the government or groups of interested doctors, and divest ourselves of the immense responsibilities of running these big organizations." – H.B. Dehqani-Tafti, The Hard Awakening, (New York: The Seabury Press, 1981), pp. 20-21.

Chapter 9~The Threshold of Asian Modernity: Letter No. 5

However, the action of the American Presbyterians, while it kept them from persecution on the scale suffered by the Episcopal Church, led to the disintegration of their congregations, as we saw in Mashhad. Doubtless, personal Christian charity must be accompanied and supplemented by Christian institutional charity, such as hospitals, to see the full fruit of Christ's instruction: "Even so let your light shine before men; that they may see your good works, and glorify your Father who is in heaven." (Matthew 5:16) However, we must be careful that the life of congregations which may come into existence, partly because of the witness radiating from a Christian charitable institution, is not so dependent on the institution that if and when the institution closes the congregation can no longer survive.

Heartland of the Middle East

CHAPTER 10

ON THE WAY TO TEHRAN

Homeward-Bound Letter No. 6
Tehran, Iran
November 18, 1975

Dear Friends,

From Mashhad, Iran on our way toward the Hyrcanian Sea (the ancient name of the Caspian Sea) we traveled west in a valley some 15 to 20 miles wide between two parallel arms of the Elburz Mountains, the major range being on our left. Here was more "big-sky farming" country but this time in western Khorasan province. This province is the Midwest of Iran. At least, it is one Midwest. Some might reasonably think the irrigation potential of the Reza Shah Pahlavi Dam on the Dez River (see picture on page 109) may swing the balance in favor of Khuzistan Province, in the southwest, as the agricultural center of the country. But here, the roads are good. The towns are prosperous. The prospects are bright.[1]

East of the city of Gorgan the road goes over a pass which crosses the northern-most arm of the Elburz, thus bringing one into the Caspian Sea coastal region, the littoral. Most of Iran is fertile but barren except where adequate water has allowed agriculture to work its miracle. Thus to drop into the area in which the climate is influenced by the Caspian is to enter a fascinating green-belt of forests and naturally verdant flora. The roof styles suddenly change and become gabled, reflecting the increased rainfall, up to sixty inches per year. Population dramatically increases, reflecting the greater ease of winning a living from the soil, the nearby fishing industry and the profitable tourism that is based on the lovely Caspian shore.

Friends in Kabul, Afghanistan, had asked us to deliver letters for them. One of the letters was for a Full-Gospel missionary in Gorgan. I looked forward to the contact which could give us insights not to be gained in any other way. A phone call revealed that neither the missionary nor his local-preacher associate were in town. However, the local preacher's wife kindly sent Kurshid, her husband's assistant, to show us the way to the house. Kurshid had been converted from Islam only a few years previously. Though he knew no English, and our broken, meager Persian knew nothing at all of the Caspian dialects, with good will and humor all around, his directions, assisted liberally by animated gestures, led us shortly to the only church building of any kind in Gorgan, a thriving city of well over 100,000.

The unique missionary church in Gorgan

Our hostess showed warm and sincere hospitality, phoning repeatedly to try, though unsuccessfully, to locate an American engineer friend I thought might be working in the city. Giving us Turkish coffee and sweets, she invited us to stay for lunch. Though we really didn't have time to accept the invitation for lunch, the visit gave us some of the insights for which we had hoped. The small congregation was, with few exceptions, made up of converts from Islam, reflecting, perhaps, the greater openness of the Shia Muslims compared with the Sunnis.[2] It also reflected the warm and capable ministry of the preacher and his wife. Protesting the cold formality of the Armenian Church of Isfahan, which they had left, they exuded warmth and friendliness. She speaks three languages (Armenian, Persian, and English) while her husband speaks five.

They used cassette recorders as well as literature to supplement their personal contacts. The literature-display window of the small church building in Gorgan attracts a steady flow of the curious and the interested. They are using the relatively free atmosphere of present-day Iran to introduce Muslims to Christ.[3] It would have been interesting and instructive to have had more contact with them.

Chapter 10~On the Way to Tehran: Letter No. 6

The shortest route from Mashhad to Tehran does not touch the Caspian shore, but having come so far, the twenty-mile digression seemed reasonable to us. So from Gorgan we went to Babol and from thence due north to Babolsar on the Caspian. It was a cold, blustery, overcast day. The Caspian Sea moderates the cold sweeping down from Russia so the winds were not the bone-chilling variety we'd experienced in Mashhad. Still, the wind was uncomfortably cold and Jonathan and I were of one mind: the water temperature did not invite a swim!

Jonathan, looking north from the south shore of the Caspian Sea.

Babolsar is a thriving summer resort town. The beach is built up for some two miles with small rental huts. Large development tracts are studded with hundreds of expensive summer homes for Tehranites, and Iranis from further south, who seek surcease from the summer's heat and who have the means to migrate north.

Had circumstances permitted I would have elected to go further west to a sturgeon fishing area to savor the atmosphere of a Caspian fishing town and perhaps taste a bit of caviar. It would also have been fascinating to have visited a Caspian tea plantation area. As it was, we were thankful for a half-hour's drive and stroll on the broad beach at Babolsar. By the way, in ancient times the Caspian was known as the Hyrcanian Sea, after an Aryan tribe of that name. They were displaced by the Caspian tribe whose name is now memorialized in that of the sea.

In addition to the fishing industry and its value as a resort area, the Caspian is important also as a sea route. However, for Iran, it in no way rivals the importance of the Persian Gulf as an artery of trade. "For example, in 1970/71 the total imports at the Caspian Sea ports amounted to less than one-eighth of those at the Persian Gulf ports; the exports from the Caspian Sea ports amounted to about one-sixth of those from the Persian Gulf ports."[4]

Also, for me it would have been extremely interesting to have gone east and then north, crossing the Gorgan River for a look at the defensive wall which Alexander the Great built there. Neither J.R. Hamilton nor W.W. Tarn mention that wall in their well-known studies of Alexander. Jan Myrdal makes only passing reference to it in his Gates to Asia, but in the Archaeological Museum in Tehran it shows clearly on a map of exploration in the Gorgan region.

Happy for our brief visit to the Caspian, we drove from Babolsar to Amol, gateway to one of the passes to Tehran from the north through the main Elburz mountain range. It was our firm decision to go through the Elburz by day to savor the passage to the full. Arriving at Amol about an hour before sundown and seeing several "towns" on the map between Amol and the summit, we thought we might as well redeem the time by driving till the sun began to set. Those "towns" proved to be nothing more than local beaneries with a naked light bulb or two hanging from the trees near the road. There were no rooms for rent and it was too cold to just sleep in the Jeep unless we unpacked a lot of bedding. So, willy-nilly, we drove over the Elburz at night, albeit a moonlit night except for several long patches of intense fog. The upper reaches were blessed with snow of some three inches along the road and a glaze of ice on the road—to make traveling more exciting. Seventeen tunnels later we arrived in downtown Tehran at about 11:00 p.m. Having seen two wrecks and a lot of reckless driving that could easily have caused more grief, we were especially glad to find rather ordinary quarters in, ironically, The Majestic Hotel!

Tehran should be grateful for both the Caspian Sea and the Elburz Mountains. In winter the freezing Russian gales are tempered by the warmth of the Caspian and largely blocked by the east-west Elburz chain, whose highest peak, Mt. Damavand, reaches 18,406 feet. Thus the Russian gales are prevented from turning Tehran into a deep freeze. These two natural features account for the marked difference between the climate in Mashhad and Tehran. In summer they play a reverse role, providing cool relief from the parched Iranian Plateau.

By invitation, for the next three nights, we set up our cots in a crowded Operation-Mobilization dormitory, where we enjoyed warm and generous hospitality. The following three nights we enjoyed the warm welcome of the Bob Staley home, friends from former years in Lahore. Our free time was used for servicing the Jeep, book hunting, visiting the Central Bank to see the fabulous Crown Jewels of Iran, a visit to the workshops of the Museum of Art and two trips to the Archaeological Museum. It was refreshing beyond words to pick up mail in Tehran and to visit even briefly with Gerry by phone.

Chapter 10~On the Way to Tehran: Letter No. 6

This photo, from northern Tehran, shows the snow on the southern skirts of Mt. Damavand, in the Elburz Mt. Range. These mountains intercept the Arctic cold weather from the north thus preventing unbearably cold weather in Tehran.

Of the many fascinating artifacts in the Archaeological Museum, two were of special interest to us. Isaiah recorded a vision which had been given to him of God on his throne. Concerning the angelic attendants around God's throne called Seraphim, Isaiah says, "each one had six wings; with twain he covered his face." (Isaiah 6:2) On the eastern end of the northern wall on the ground floor of the museum we saw the massive 6th century B.C. bas-relief taken from the Treasury

building at Persepolis. I had deliberately searched for this among the surfeit of displays because of one detail I had read of it. Sylvia A. Matheson says of the relief that it shows "Darius the Great on his throne, with his son, Crown Prince Xerxes, standing immediately behind him, and in front, beyond two small incense burners, a Median official, probably the 'Chiliarch' in charge of the Treasury, and also Commander of the Army, holding his hand before his mouth in a gesture of respect."5

I found the bas-relief a thrilling commentary on Isaiah's description. I thought of Samuel saying to God, "Speak my Lord for thy servant heareth." And of James' exhortation, "Let every man be swift to hear, slow to speak." The Achaemenids could teach us much about proper decorum in the presence of the True King of Kings and Lord of Lords.[6]

At the front entrance to the museum stands a decapitated black basalt royal statue. It is immediately arresting because it not only has the typical cuneiform writing of the Achaemenids but is also covered with Egyptian hieroglyphics. Fortunately, on a nearby bulletin board we found the explanation: "Stone statue of Darius the Great (Reign 522-486 B.C.) discovered at Susa 1972." The statue shows the king dressed in the Persian fashion but in the same pose as Egyptian Pharaohs. This Egyptian style is explained in the cuneiform inscription: "This is the stone statue of Darius the Great ordered to be made in Egypt." On the base, we could see inscribed in Egyptian hieroglyphics: "The King of Lower and Upper Egypt, Master of the ritual accomplishments, Daryaoesh. May he live forever!" This statue with another one (similar?) guarded the monumental entrance of the palace of Darius at Susa. Here we had come face-to-face with biblical realities in a fresh and most impressive form.

The king who confirmed and enforced Cyrus' decree for the rebuilding of the temple (Ezra chapter 6), the extent of the Achaemenid Empire claimed by his successor (Esther 1:1) and the glory of the Achaemenian palace at Shushan (Susa) (Esther 1:5-7) all stood confirmed and indelibly impressed on our awareness by just this one statue and its inscriptions. The stones in the great museum at Tehran stood as testifying witnesses (Joshua 24:27, Luke 19:40) and we rejoiced in their testimony.

We hope we will be able to share more with you from these great kings when we visit some of their centers of power a few days from now. Until then.

In the name of the King of Kings,
Lee and Jonathan

---

1 The adverse economic consequences of the Khomeini revolution are highlighted by contrasting statistics. In 1980 the exiled Shah evaluated the economic progress which had taken place during his reign. He wrote, "When Mossadegh was in power, Iran's budget was around $400 million. Our last budget was $57 billion, of which approximately $20 billion came from oil revenues and the rest from taxes that the people could now afford; in 1963 our per capita income was $174, in 1978, the last year of my reign, it was $2,540. And all of this was accomplished at a time of great population growth, from 27 million in 1968 to 36 million in 1978. And our social programs were developing under the White Revolution at a remarkable rate." – Mohammad Reza Pahlavi, Answer to History, (New York: Stein and Day Publishers, 1980), p. 176.

Chapter 10~On the Way to Tehran: Letter No. 6

In stark contrast, "for several weeks after Iraq's intensive series of attacks on tankers in April and May [of 1984], Iranian oil exports dropped to about 500,000-600,000 barrels a day, about one quarter of Iran's normal wartime exports. The drop was artificially steep because Iran was slow to offer discounts to compensate for the sudden increase in insurance rates, and Iran's oil exports have since recovered. Still, the figures must be sobering for Tehran's leaders to ponder. If reduced to such a level of exports for any extended period, Iran would have trouble paying even for food imports." – Michael Sterner, The Iran–Iraq War, Foreign Affairs, Fall 1984, p. 134.

    Khomeini has insisted on pursuing this war after the invader has been thrown completely out of Iran and in the face of many pleas from Iraq for peace. He and his leaders, therefore, are certainly responsible for the economic consequences from this painfully protracted war. Those consequences are, obviously, severe. "The confiscation of its foreign assets, the war with Iraq, the virtual cessation of oil production, and the flight of the middle class abroad or into hiding brought the modern sector of the Iranian economy to a juddering halt." – Paul Johnson, Modern Times The World From the Twenties to the Eighties, (New York: Harper & Row Publishers, 1983), p. 708.

2 Shi'ism is a protest movement in Islam that, on one hand, may protest by showing itself more zealous than the "orthodox" or, on the other hand, by being more open to non-Islamic ideas. Other factors are also operative. William McElwee Miller points out one of them when he says, "the Shi'ite theologians had long ago maintained that personal investigation is obligatory in matters which concern the fundamentals of religion." – What is the Baha'i Faith?, (Grand Rapids: Wm. B. Eerdmans Publishing Co., 1977), p. 99.

    Another factor may be the desire for joy and for a saviour which is obvious even to foreign observers. "It must be confessed that there is something particularly sad about Persian Shi'ism. The intensity of grief, with which the Muharram ceremonies commemorating the martyrdom of Hussein are marked, is something no spectator can ever forget. The black turbans of the mullahs and the black chadors of Persian women combine to emphasize this sense of sadness. As a nation the Persians have too often looked back from under foreign or native despotism to a golden age when their country, one of the oldest geographical entities in the world, was the object of universal fear and respect. As believers they have been waiting for a thousand years for the reappearance of the imam, the liberator and saviour." – Mohamed Heikal, Iran: The Untold Story, (New York: Pantheon Books, 1982), p. 82.

    Keddie points out that, "the Shi'is, who originally had few doctrinal differences with the Sunnis, were, as an oppositional group, more open to outside influences." – Nikki R. Keddie, Roots of Revolution An Interpretive History of Modern Iran, (New Haven and London: Yale University Press, 1981), p. 6. However, as Keddie goes on to document, that openness resulted in major development of "natural law rationalism" based on acceptance of Greek philosophy and an allegorical interpretation of the Quran to accommodate it. (cf. Ibid, pp. 18-19) It is this "natural law rationalism," along with other factors, which forms the basis for the cooperation of large and powerful segments of contemporary Islam with Communism.

    On the other hand, until very recent times, another factor in what seems to be a greater openness to the Gospel of Christ among Shi'ites may be the greater spiritual emphasis enforced on that branch of Islam contrasted with the greater political emphasis in the Sunni branch. As Frye remarks, "the Shi'ites, denied political leadership in Islam, concerned themselves more with spiritual leadership. The office of caliph as political leader was distinguished from that of imam, or religious leader." – Richard N. Frye, Iran, (New York: Henry Holt and Company, 1953), p. 16. Confirming all this, there seems to be a greater turning to Christ among Shi'ite Muslims from Iran among immigrants and refugees from Muslim countries than those with Sunni background. Of course, the Shi'ite branch of Islam has now taken an extremely prominent political role. Regarding the political propensities of Shi'ite Islam, one should read James A. Bill, Resurgent Islam, Foreign Affairs, Fall 1984, pp. 108-127.

3 It was relatively free when compared with Sassanian Iran (See Letter No. 7, paragraphs 9 and 10) and certainly when compared with present-day Iran under Khomeini.

4 Rouhollah K. Ramazani, The Persian Gulf, Iran's Role, (Charlottesville: University Press of Virginia, 1972), p. 80.

5 Sylvia A. Matheson, Persia: An Archaeological Guide, (London: Faber, 1976), pp. 40-41.

6 In the biblical concept, putting the hand over one's mouth is sometimes a mark of astonishment (Job 21:5) and/or reverence (Isaiah 52:15).

Heartland of the Middle East

CHAPTER 11

HALF THE WORLD

The Setting: Before Isfahan permanently became part of the Shia Muslim world, it was a battleground to determine whether it would be Shia or Sunni. For a time it was controlled by the Turkish ruler Suleiman the Magnificent, who took over Iraq and penetrated as far as Tabriz and Isfahan. *"Suleiman had his eastern edge problems, too, namely the Safavids with their claims to Islamic supremacy. The unruly borderlands between the two Islamic powers defied Ottoman control."*[1] Following the definitive defeat of Suleiman's forces in 1529 at Vienna, Austria, Isfahan was no longer threatened with a takeover by Sunni Islam. *"In 1529 after conquering the whole Balkan Peninsula, with the exception of Greece, the Ottoman army was poised at the gates of Vienna to deliver the death blow. At that critical moment, the Iranian Safavids, whose capital was Isfahan, attacked the Ottomans' eastern border making it urgently necessary for the Ottomans to move their troops from Vienna to face the new peril."*[2]

Homeward-Bound Letter No. 7
Isfahan, Iran
November 21, 1975

Dear Friends,

According to an ancient saying about Isfahan, on November 19 we had encompassed half the world. The saying goes, *Isfahan-nisf jahan*, which, being interpreted, means "Isfahan is half the world." Does that truism reflect pride based only on extreme parochialism or on something more significant?

Though situated on a high inland desert plateau, it has not suffered the isolation that breeds parochialism. On the contrary, as Roger Stevens points out, the fame of this fabled oasis drew many to make the arduous journey thither. "What incredulity must have assailed the seventeenth-century traveler as he lumbered by slow camel train across these bleak and barren uplands, churning up the fine white dust on his way to what he had been told was the most splendid city, and the most sophisticated and luxurious court in the world? Would it not prove another mirage? And then quite suddenly the miracle occurred. Coming from the south, he swung down from a barren ridge and there it was, only the towers of the mosques and the palace gates visible over the high chenars. Soon, like John Fryer, he was crossing 'a most magnificent bridge with arches over our heads and on both sides rails and galleries to view the river.' … Contrast to the surrounding desert, is what gives the place its exceptional quality. One has the impression of a flourishing community which has evolved its own superlative expression in art and architecture, pressed round by its ring of green, watered as it were by an unseen hand, living its own self-contained and self-sufficient life, shut off by mountains and deserts from the rest of the world, haughty, a little arrogant perhaps, but pulsating with vitality."3

It isn't just "contrast to the surrounding desert" which "gives the place its exceptional quality," as Stevens suggests. For one thing, there is an enchanting beauty about the place that has captivated its citizens and visitors alike. The awareness of that unique beauty is perhaps reflected in some of the names one encounters in the city. However, those names and the mystical beauty of the Safavid sections of the city may mask from the uninformed the horrible tortures, sufferings, and injustices which have taken place through the centuries in Isfahan. For example, Tamerlane in 1397 had 70,000 citizens of the city beheaded for rebelling against the atrocities of his troops. Then in a ten-year period, from 1604-1614, between 60,000 and 70,000 families of Armenian and Georgian Christians were forcibly deported from their homes in the Caspian littoral to this desert oasis under the dictatorial rule of the Safavid king, Shah Abbas. I want to share more with you about those deportees, but before that, a bit about those intriguing names to which I alluded.

A look at some of the names in Isfahan may make us wonder if the Safavid town planners were reading the Book of Revelation when they laid out portions of the city. The river (which, of course, the planners did not lay out) is called the River of Life! While it does not reflect the far greater concept of the River of Life mentioned in Revelation 22:1, it does reflect the very obvious ecological fact that all agriculture here has, through the centuries, been dependent upon the river. Thus, in a very real way, the river has given life to the city.

Just how dependent life is on the river was sadly illustrated in the years 1868-1870 when the rains failed. During the ensuing famine, 12,000 perished in Isfahan.4 It was a keen awareness of the role of the river which gave birth to "the custom of the Armenians at Epiphanytide to conduct a very solemn and gorgeous ceremony of Blessing the Waters of the Zayandehrud River in Isfahan."5 Under the capable administration of the present Shah of Iran, in 1953 a tunnel was completed after five years' work which brings part of the waters of the Karun River over the watershed and adds it to the flow of the Zayandehrud. Thus, theoretically, such a catastrophe cannot happen again.

Now, back to those names. On the south bank of the Zayandehrud (The River of Life) is the street Khyaban-e-Dalan-e-Behisht, which means The Avenue Which Leads to the Threshold of Heaven or Threshold of Heaven Avenue! On the other side of the River of Life is Khyaban-e-Bagh-e-Jannat, i.e., The Avenue Which Leads to the Garden of Heaven!

In the south part of the area called Julfa is a street named Khyaban-e-Hoseynabad, i.e., The Avenue Which Leads to the Abode of Beauty! Another street is Khyaban-e-Shahzadeh Ebrahim, i.e., The Avenue of the Royal Heirs of Abraham! (Cer-

Chapter 11~Half the World: Letter No. 7

tainly they are the only ones who can set foot on the threshold of heaven's door! cf. Romans 4:1-12).

To reach the ultimate, but by no means exhausting the examples, there are two parallel streets with extremely notable names. The first is Behisht Aieen Avenue which means The Avenue Which is the Mirror of Heaven. Appropriately enough, just two streets away is Hasht Behisht Boulevard, The Boulevard of the Eight Heavens! As I did, you may find it surprisingly harmonious with such striking nomenclature that the four royal gardens established by order of King Shah Abbas were made accessible by a street still called The Avenue of the Four Gardens and that "the water channels which ran the whole length of the avenue down to the river were faced with onyx."6

This photo was taken near Naqsh-e-Rustam in Iran. Near the road, just behind our jeep, are two tapering square ancient fire altars. Though now inoperative, for centuries they constantly kept flames alive by burning natural gas which made its way to the surface at this point. In the immediate foreground are great stone slabs where human bodies were placed for birds to strip the skeletons clean. Those procedures were religious in nature and are venerated in the Bagavand Gita, Iran's oldest religious document. This photo emphasizes the activity for which Ateshgah Avenue in Isfahan was named.

When you visit Isfahan, just to keep you from supposing, against all sound theology, that you have unwittingly stumbled into heaven, a further glance at the map should keep you headed in the right direction. One street leading west is Ateshgah Avenue (Fire Avenue).7 The dear people living near the street are, sadly, misdirected. Their leader, one Ahmad Mirza from Qaidian, India, claimed during his life that he was himself the Christ!

Heartland of the Middle East

On the other hand, it would be admirable if the celestial names on a lot of the streets in Isfahan should reflect the citizens' desire to ultimately inherit heaven. Unfortunately, history doesn't seem to indicate that all this represented a yearning for heaven. For instance, Hasht Behesht used to have gardens full of nightingales, "which Chardin thought made for the delights of love."[8]

Importance of Isfahan

In addition to its enchanting beauty, Isfahan was and is important because of its strategic location. It was the terminus of important southern routes crossing the Iranian plateau from India. On the other hand, it was the staging point for caravans wishing to go to India from southwest Iran or from southern Mesopotamia. Isfahan is centrally situated. Being well away from any border, and yet equally accessible to nearly any point on the perimeter, several times it was chosen as the capital of Iran.

Naqsh-e Jahan Square at night

Of the buildings, so justly famed, which make the largest contribution to the magical beauty of the city as it stands today, most were built during the reign of Shah Abbas, the fifth and greatest of the Safavid kings, who chose the city in 1598 for his capital. If you stand, as we did, on a winter evening in the gardens of the great city square and watch the Lutfullah Mosque to the west and across the square fade into deep shadow, you will keenly sense the mysterious spell Isfahan casts upon those who stop even briefly to savor it. Shah Abbas' architects laid out the square on a scale even grander than Red Square in Moscow! The sunset highlights the minarets of the great Royal Mosque while at the same time playing magic with the colors of the gleaming tiles of the great Iwan of the Shaikh Lutfullah mosque.

Chapter 11~Half the World: Letter No. 7

But I must turn from thoughts of architectural virtuosity and its magic to share a bit about those Christian deportees whom I mentioned earlier.

Antioch of Syria was the center from which the Gospel spread east and north, as well as west and north. The latter is better known because of the record in the book of Acts. Two things eventually led to the eastern churches' (collectively they became known as The Church of The East) estrangement from Antioch, and finally from any living relationship with Western Christianity or Christendom, into which it had largely developed by the time of the rupture. Antioch was a new city established by Seleucus I as a capital of the Seleucid Empire. The Seleucid domestic policy was firmly based on a program of unification through Hellenization. Naturally, the capital was, therefore, Greek-speaking, even in the Roman period when the church took root there and became a great center of evangelism. The great Christian centers in the east, on the other hand, such as Edessa, Nisibis and Haran were Aramaic speaking. The first strain between the eastern and western churches was, consequently, a linguistic one. Another factor which led to separation was political. From 224-651 A.D. Iran was governed by the Sassanians, whom the Byzantine Romans could not conquer. A more or less constant state of war persisted along the Euphrates frontier between these two great empires.

Administrative Center of Ali Qapu Palace in Naqsh-e Jahan Square

The Sassanians made Zoroastrianism the state religion, which in itself put Christianity in Iran at a great disadvantage. Thus, whenever Persian Christians reached out to make contact with their brethren in Antioch or other western centers they were suspected of indulging in subversive activity against the Sassanian Empire by keeping contacts with an enemy state. This suspicion led in turn to persecution for the Christians under Sassanian rule. The official rescript of Emperor Shahpur

II, justifying his putting to death over one hundred Christians, alleged that the Christians "share the sentiments of our enemy Caesar."[9]

In this kind of charged cultural and political atmosphere it is no wonder that formal division came over subtle doctrinal distinctions which were drawn during the Nestorian Controversy. It was that controversy which ostensibly led to formal separation of the churches of the east. Final separation was decided on at an eastern synod in 424 A.D. which elevated the eastern "Catholicos to the status of a Patriarch, thus freeing the Church from the rule of the Patriarch of Antioch under whom they had been until that time."[10]

Ceiling detail in audience hall of Ali Qapu Palace

The eastern Patriarch had his headquarters on the Euphrates at Selucia-Ctesiphon, the capital of the Sassanian Empire, just as the Patriarch of Rome had his headquarters on the Tiber in the capital of the Roman Empire. Both the theology and the organization of these official churches of east and west were by this time far from the heavenly pattern (Hebrews 8:5). Yet in both east and west there were

Chapter 11~Half the World: Letter No. 7

Under extremely difficult photographic conditions, this view shows some of the great devotional architectural intricacy displayed inside the cathedral.

many honest and devoted communicants who sincerely tried to serve Christ. As loyal followers of Christ died in the west from imperial persecutions before the Edict of Toleration in 323 A.D., so God's people suffered under Imperial Sassanian persecutions in the east which began in 341 A.D. under King Shapur II. Over a century later persecution still raged. Under Emperor Yazdagird II a fierce persecution took place and the victims from a wide area were gathered on August 24 and 25 in 446 A.D. near present Kirkuk. "The way in which one of the Christian women, Shirin, and her two sons met their death so touched the King's officer in charge of the proceedings that he too confessed faith in Christ and on 25 September was himself crucified."[11]

Centuries later, Shah Abbas found a community of Armenian Christians, descendants of these courageous martyrs, living in Julfa in the extreme northwest corner of Iran. He was attracted by their diligence and acumen in trade and industry. He felt their presence in large numbers would help ensure the economic vitality of his new capital at Isfahan. So in 1604 he forced some twelve thousand families to move to an adjacent area southwest of Isfahan.[12] One method of coercion was seizing and closing their sources of irrigation water.[13] In their new location, the Armenians had to build their own city. In memory of their old home, they called their new town Julfa, which eventually merged into Isfahan. In their new home the Armenians prospered, in some cases too much for their own good. "Their industry appears to have provoked a certain amount of jealousy, for Frye tells us that at the end of the century they were forbidden to enter the city with their servants 'bearing after them their Kelyans, or Glass Vessels out of which they smoke tobacco,' but were allowed to appear only as merchants."[14]

The Vank Armenian Cathedral

However, one advantage Shah Abbas bestowed was official permission to build church buildings. Today in Julfa, the Armenian Cathedral (built between 1606 and 1654) and several other church buildings are the focal points of the religious activity of this ancient Christian community. They were zealous to provide scripture for their people and in this interest installed the first successful printing press in the Middle East. The original press, type molds, and many samples of early scripture portions in Armenian are on display in the very modern museum building in the Cathedral compound.

Chapter 11~Half the World: Letter No. 7

There is also a very ancient Jewish community in Isfahan but many, if not most, of the less affluent have migrated to Israel. We learned more about them on the Wednesday evening during our stay in Isfahan when we were invited to a midweek fellowship meeting of the Church of England. The Church Missionary Society had established a mission hospital some sixty years earlier in Isfahan. The Anglican church building is in the hospital compound. The local Irani Anglican preacher is a long-time convert from Judaism who gave us brief but interesting insights into the current situation in the local Jewish community.[15]

The Armenian Museum in Isfahan

Also, there are now hundreds of Americans living in Isfahan. Their numbers are expected to increase to thousands shortly. One of the world's largest military helicopter schools is located here. The Americans, employees of Bell Helicopter, form the multi-talented faculty of the school. They have brought, temporarily at least, a sampling of American heterogeneous denominational religious life to Isfahan. In a book shop we saw meeting notices for three different groups.

All for now. Thanks for letting us share a bit with you. We hope we all may one day drink from the Real Zayandehrud!

With love,
Lee and Jonathan

P.S. The military significance of Isfahan, which was highlighted by the Bell Helicopter University, will be carried forward by a much more ominous activity by the current Iranian government.

This prediction is seen in a current events update: "A confidential report by the United Nations atomic agency, seen by *The Wall Street Journal*, said Iran had started producing uranium metal on Feb. 6 at a nuclear facility in Isfahan that is under the agency's inspection." – Laurence Norman, *Iran Makes Uranium Metal in Breech of Nuclear Deal*, The Wall Street Journal, February 11, 2021, p. A1.

Though it may seem that Isfahan is located in an out-of-the-way area in Iran, as this news break makes clear, Isfahan is continuing its significant role in international affairs.

The average people of Isfahan are fascinated by competitive activity between pigeons, which are housed and fed in elaborate multi-story pigeon towers, like these which rise well above the common sky line of Isfahan.

---

1 Donald N. Wilber, Iran, Past and Present, (Princeton NJ: Princeton University Press, 1963), p. 63.
2 Jane Burbank and Frederick Cooper, Empires in World History, (Princeton, NJ: Princeton University Press, 2010), p. 144.
3 Roger Stevens, The Land of the Great Sophy, (London: Methuen & Co. Ltd., 1962), p. 182.
4 Robin E. Waterfield, Christians in Persia, (London: George Allen & Unwin Ltd., 1973), p. 115.
5 Robin E. Waterfield, Christians in Persia, (London: George Allen & Unwin Ltd., 1973), p. 67.
6 Roger Stevens, The Land of the Great Sophy, (London: Methuen & Co. Ltd., 1962), p. 185.
7 Ateshgah means "place of fire." The perpetual flame at such places was fueled by natural gas which made its way to the surface. Those places of perpetual fire were dignified by building a tapering square altar around the orifice from which the gas exited from the earth. Such places were revered. Please see the picture on page 83 of the Ateshgah at Naqsh-e-Rustam.
8 Roger Stevens, The Land of the Great Sophy, (London: Methuen & Co. Ltd., 1962), p. 187.

Chapter 11~Half the World: Letter No. 7

---

9   Robin E. Waterfield, <u>Christians in Persia</u>, (London: George Allen & Unwin Ltd., 1973), p. 19.
10 Robin E. Waterfield, <u>Christians in Persia</u>, (London: George Allen & Unwin Ltd., 1973), p. 23.
11 Robin E. Waterfield, <u>Christians in Persia</u>, (London: George Allen & Unwin Ltd., 1973), p. 26.
12 An additional comment on this may be of interest. Frye points out that Shah Abbas had a "policy to mix population and separate possibly troublesome peoples. ... The policy of moving possibly rebellious tribes or groups of people from one part of the country to another is, of course, an ancient one in the history of Iran." – Richard N. Frye, <u>Iran,</u> (New York: Henry Holt and Company, 1953), pp. 10-13. While the forced migration of the Julfa Christians may have been carried out under that policy, it seems the main consideration was the contribution Shah Abbas hoped they would make to the success of his new capital.
13 A later reading note made me realize Shah Abbas had been, relatively speaking, very lenient with those Christians. "But, for all his genius and many sterling qualities, Abbas, like many absolute rulers, possessed a streak of excessive cruelty that placed him in the same league as his infamous contemporary, Ivan the Terrible of Russia. It was this weakness in his make-up that contributed largely to the later decline and fall of the Safavids. Fearing that his sons might sooner or later attempt to usurp the throne, he ordered the death of his eldest child and blinded his two remaining sons. Abbas was often quoted as claiming he would gladly kill 100 children to reign alone for a single day. There seemed no reason to doubt that he meant it." – Jon A. Teta, <u>Iran in Pictures</u>, (New York: Sterling Publishing Co., 1973), pp. 29-30.
14 Roger Stevens, <u>The Land of the Great Sophy</u>, (London: Methuen & Co. Ltd., 1962), p. 186.
15 This mission hospital compound with its church and bishop's house became one of the focal points of persecution of Christians in Iran following the Khomeini revolution. Those who wish to inform themselves about this persecution, should begin by reading, H.B. Dehqani-Tafti, <u>The Hard Awakening</u>, (New York: The Seabury Press, 1981). Since Dehqani-Tafti has been mentioned, the reader should also know of his delightful book, <u>Design of My World</u>, (London: United Society for Christian Literature, 1959). In his book Dehqani-Tafti gives unique insights into the nature of Islam and into living in an Islamic society.

Heartland of the Middle East

Chapter 12

World Capitals

Homeward-Bound Letter No. 8-A
Shushan the Palace
November 27, 1975

Dear Friends,

As we mentioned in our previous letter, if Isfahan is half the world, according to the proud boast of that city, we could say with more justification we had reached the long-term epicenter of the world just northeast of Shiraz. On the way from Isfahan to Shiraz, I confess, my excitement picked up, and perhaps my pulse rate did too, when we passed a sign stating that we were crossing into the province of Fars. In ancient times the spelling and pronunciation of Fars was often represented by the letters "Pars." The Parsee communities in India and Pakistan, preserving that old spelling in their name, advertise both their lineage and their place of origin. But as we crossed that border my thoughts were not centered on the Parsees but on Cyrus, Darius and Xerxes (the Persian form of the Hebrew Ahasuerus) and the part they had played in the great plan of God.

About 3:30 in the afternoon of November 22nd, we turned off the main road to Shiraz and drove four miles to Pasargadae (literally the Camp of the Persians), the capital city of Cyrus the Great. The royal tribe of the Persian people "was that of Pasargadae. When we find that the same name is assigned to their earliest capital by the majority of Greek writers, we might assume that the capital was so named from the tribe."[1] However, Olmstead is right, Pasargadae was what the Greeks called it. It has not yet been discovered what the Persians themselves called their first imperial capital. The head of the Archaeological Department of Fars, Dr. Ali Sami, claims Alexander shipped all the royal documents to Greece where they were destroyed after passages valuable to the Greeks had been translated. The Persian scholars, according to this authority, were then killed so they could not record anything again from memory. In this context, the Persian name for Pasargadae may never be known.

The mystery about the name didn't reduce or dampen our excitement nor attenuate our awe in the least as we examined the ruins of the first capital of Iran's Achaemenid Empire. In spite of the extensive destruction which Pasargadae has sustained in the twenty-five centuries since it was built, its ruins still convey an imperial aura to the thoughtful beholder.

The tomb of Cyrus the Great at Pasargadae

In contrast to Persepolis, which Alexander the Great contemptuously burned, Pasargadae was given his protection. He deeply admired Cyrus the Great and restored his tomb after it had been molested by robbers trying to carry off the gold sarcophagus. The destruction of Pasargadae was mostly the work of Muslim Arabs who carted off the pillar drums to be cut down for millstones and who used much of the other material for mosque construction. Their gross ignorance kept them from even greater damage. They thought the tomb of Cyrus the Great was the tomb of the mother of Solomon, the great king of Israel! Out of honor to Solomon they not only tried to protect the tomb but used some pillar drums from the palaces to build a crude fence around it!

One of the most interesting of the remaining bas-reliefs in Pasargadae is one thought by many competent scholars to be of Cyrus himself, though the cuneiform inscription which was above the bas-relief till the eighteenth century was, unfortunately, broken off and destroyed before it could be copied for translation. It shows Cyrus wearing a two-horned helmet, the horns being rendered in the curved Egyptian style. This is extremely arresting in view of the symbolism in the book of Daniel for the Achaemenid Empire (Daniel 8:3-4).

§

Chapter 12~World Capitals: Letter No. 8-A

IRANIAN GLORY THROUGH PHOTOS OF PERSEPOLIS

The organizational capability of the Achaemenian-Iranian Empire[2] first achieved its spectacular success from work carried out in Pasargadae. Even more so, it grew from the work done in Persepolis, which became its central administrative nerve center.[3] It was dynamic—staffed by creative, obedient and adaptive personnel, which, combined, made the military and administrative miracle of the Achaemenian Empire possible. Thus, its emperors were able to reign "from India even unto Ethiopia, over a hundred and seven and twenty provinces," as the biblical book of Esther tells us in 1:1.

Everywhere we looked during the time Jonathan and I criss-crossed our way up and down, east to west through Iran, we were stunned by the newly developing obvious potential of the country. Even within its limited modern boundaries, clearly, Iran could reasonably hope to emulate the amazing proficiency and professionalism of their great ancestors, the Achaemenids. The fulfillment of such a vision was delayed and nearly totally derailed by the Shia-Islamic Khomeini Revolution. Immediately following those eight years of revolutionary war, Iran could only hope, while surviving tenuously, to secure its then current borders.

Even as the Iranian population recovered from the massive losses it sustained during its war for revolutionary independence, its leaders began to see ways for expansion. One very strategic step was to strengthen Bashar al-Assad, a renowned Shiite leader, in his fight to retain rule over Syria, his horribly wounded country. Their alliance with al-Bashar gave Iran significant access and influence all the way to the Mediterranean!

That gain was amplified by Iran supporting powerful rebels who, following the fall of Hussein (the dictator of Iraq), were trying to take control of Iraq. By the total pull-out of American military forces from Iraq during the Obama administration, the resulting Iraqi weakness made Iranian influence even more threatening.

Subsequently, Iran is currently flexing its muscles by supporting the Houthi rebellion/offensive against Saudi Arabia's control over Yemen. Just as the month of March 2021 came to its end, China and Iran announced a twenty-five year close association which will give Iran an enormous stable market for its oil, while allowing it to negate much of the damage it has sustained through economic limitations imposed by the U.S. By accessing China's enormous reserves of dollars, Iran may have successfully broken some of the other major bonds imposed by America.[4]

It has just been announced that China is creating digital currency, a first for a major economy. "Cyber yuan will let Beijing track spending in real time, pose challenge to dollar."[5]

Heartland of the Middle East

To help anyone trying to understand the mystique of Iranian power, this chapter presents a selection of scenes from the ruins of Persepolis. It was Iran's most magnificent capital at the time of its greatest peak of power, both locally and in international affairs.

The ceremonial dual staircase leading from ground level to the floor of the great hall of audience

As you prepare to walk up the magnificent ceremonial stairway to the main level of Persepolis, you pass a multi-layered bas-relief depiction of loyal citizens coming with exotic gifts for the emperor to show their appreciation for being allowed citizenship in this magnificent empire. The stunning faithfulness and real-life

Chapter 12~World Capitals: Letter No. 8-A

accuracy of the vast multinational parade of gift-bearing, loyal and grateful citizens should move the beholder with awe for a government which was able to inspire such loyalty.

Though it has been twenty-three-hundred and fifty-one years since Alexander the Great burned this central administrative office complex, the glory of this great governmental center not only survives, but still stuns and dazzles any thoughtful person who is privileged to visit it!

The governmental and administrative work which emanated authoritatively from this center of creative control was augmented by regional nodes of authority which often were the upgraded conquered facilities of previous governments. Those centers were subsequently re-utilized by the Iranian Achaemenian Empire.

Iranian Emperors Fought the Forces of Evil

One of the reasons vast throngs of citizens in the Achaemenian Empire felt a deep sense of loyalty to the emperor, was the protection which he provided at many

levels. For example, it was possible to travel safely throughout the empire's vast area stretching from the Indus River to the Nile, east to west, and from the Black Sea to the Indian Ocean, north to south. Caravanserais were established throughout that extensive empire.

A traveling citizen, for a low fee, could spend the night safely in any one of those centers of hospitality with complete confidence. Also, mail service was provided for every city and town in the empire.

Beyond concerns of physical safety and convenience, as this bas-relief shows, the emperor himself was not immune to demonic/satanic assaults. His vulnerability is shown here by Ahriman having his claws in the lower leg of the emperor.

However, the protection of the empire from satanic attacks by Ahriman is unmistakably shown by the emperor thrusting his royal dagger into the belly of the demon.

Despite the replete empire-wide daily responsibilities for which final decisions could be made only by the emperor, here the great emperor Darius exudes calmness and confidence. His unperturbed visage expresses his assurance that demonic attacks, complicated decisions about endless civil issues, as well as settlement of disturbances at various places on the borders of the empire, would all be duly resolved with great competence.

Chapter 12~World Capitals: Letter No. 8-A

The grand ceremonial staircase

Opposite the grand ceremonial staircase, on the other side of the very broad avenue/parade ground, wide enough to accommodate military units on display, the floor pattern of the Hall of 100 Columns, empirical in its dimensions, inspires one to imagine royal receptions which undoubtedly were held at this venue.

The Hall of 100 Columns

These columns were basic elements in the oldest palace structure at Persepolis, the Apadama. To judge the height of the columns, which are nearly 79 feet tall, notice Jonathan standing by one of the base segments.

The thoughtful observer will marvel at the statistics which had to coalesce to bring this hall of columns into being. The stone, having both the beauty and strength necessary for this specific structural utilization, must have tested the knowledge and expertise of quarry operators, as well as that of Iran's best geologists. To cut each segment with such minute accuracy that the column would not be thrown askew, tells us that Iran's stone masons and architects were the most skillful in the world. To accurately and precisely cut the fluting on each segment before a column was assembled, to support the massive roof, required the artists who worked in stone to have had the most highly developed equipment and professional skills. It is a tribute to their professional competence that thirteen of those columns have stood for all the centuries subsequent to their erection in the mid sixth century B.C.!

Chapter 12~World Capitals: Letter No. 8-A

As a visitor makes his way to ascend to the main platform by use of the royal stairway, along the walls he will see an endless parade of devoted citizens bringing gifts to show their loyalty to the emperor and the empire. If you look at the vast variety of distinct head gear, it shows that those citizens had come from widely dispersed areas. Similarly, the gift of animals being led in this parade tells us of the expanse of the empire. Both one-humped and two-humped camels are on display. Humped and no humped oxen are there too. Wild animals, which have been trained for strict obedience, are being brought to the emperor. Some of the gifts were so heavy that carts were needed to convey them.

The skill of the artists working in stone is magnified by their ability to portray a 360 degree concept by using only bas-relief carving. Many of the participants in the gift parade are armed, wearing their short battle swords as they go to express their gratitude and loyalty to the emperor. Nothing could have expressed empire unity more dramatically than allowing armed citizens from areas all over the empire to come into the presence of the emperor without fear of regicide!

Chapter 12~World Capitals: Letter No. 8-A

Within the public sections of the great capital at Persepolis were also areas built and dedicated for private use by emperors, like this one especially designed for use by Darius.

§

Heartland of the Middle East

Letter 8-B

I began writing this letter day-before-yesterday evening in Shiraz, Iran, but had to leave it to make preparations for an early departure from Shiraz on November 28th. (We tried to be sure to leave Iran before the time on our tourist permits expired. Not only had winter closed western routes, but Iraq had flatly refused us permission to set foot in their country.) Tonight, we are in the very heart of the ancient country of Elam, at Susa, the Shushan of the Bible (Esther 1:2, Daniel 8:2). There is a living town here, right on the edge of the great mound of Susa, as so often is the case with the ancient *tells*, as the mounds are called by archaeologists. The modern village goes by the name of Shush, only a slight variation of the biblical name, *Shushan*. Both the biblical name and the modern one are unmistakable derivatives from the name of the chief deity of the ancient Elamites who was called In<u>shush</u>inak. The underlining emphasizes the portion of the name which is common to the biblical name "*Shushan*" and the modern name, Shush.

Daniel's tomb in Susa

Chapter 12~World Capitals: Letter No. 8-B

It is inconceivable that anyone who understands the degree of perceptive gifts God had bestowed upon Daniel would not want to see how his life had been memorialized. Both Jonathan and I were eager to visit Daniel's tomb and be enlightened by any extra-biblical information which might enhance our understanding and appreciation of such a great spokesman for God. At the tomb, because we were Christians, entrance was flatly denied by the Muslims who had usurped control of the site. That denial was not given politely, but roughly and insultingly. We could get no information about the upside-down, ice-cream-cone-like, structure at Daniel's tomb. Though grateful to God for allowing us to visit the site where he had worked so splendidly through his servant Daniel, we departed feeling we had been robbed of a significant part of our heritage.

Tomb-Temples Known as Ziggurats

Jonathan and I got a fascinating look at ancient Elam when we visited Choga Zanbil, approximately fifty kilometers from Shush near the Dez River (a tributary to the Karun River) where the largest surviving ziggurat, that has been discovered so far, stands in awesome silence.

Though not a part of my original letter, this and the next paragraph will help the reader understand the significance of Choga Zanbil for the biblical patriarchs: For example, Abraham was keenly aware that a vast region (in which his home city of Ur was located) was dominated by theological concepts which took people away from untarnished devotion to the sole God of the Universe. Though Choga Zanbil had not yet been constructed, its concepts being actively promoted were ruling theological thinking in society even in Abraham's time. He saw his trek from Haran to Palestine as a kind of exodus from the influence of the corrupt theology dominating the vast watershed of both the Euphrates and the Tigris Rivers and their tributaries.

In seeking a wife for Isaac, his son, Abraham made it clear that Isaac should not be brought under the influence of that corrupt Euphrates-Tigris theology. He said to his servant, "Thou wilt not take a wife for my son of daughters of the Canaanites among whom I dwell but thou shall go unto my country, and to my kindred, and take a wife for my son Isaac, and the servant said unto him, 'Peradventure the woman will not be willing to follow me unto this land: must I needs bring thy son again unto the land from whence thou camest?' And Abraham said unto him, 'Beware that thou bring not my son thither again. … If the woman be not willing to follow thee, thou shalt be clear from this thy oath: only thou shalt not bring my son thither again.'" (Genesis 24:3-8)

Choga Zanbil - The corrupt theology prevailing during the lifetime of the biblical patriarchs no doubt emanated from and was sustained by teachers sent out from great centers like this one at Choga Zanbil. The dimensions of Choga Zanbil are breathtaking: 345.14 feet long on each side and 173.88 feet high at its peak.

Later, the same rigid, uncompromising theological rules guided Isaac's search for a wife for his son Jacob. Then Isaac said to his son, "'Thou shalt not take a wife of the daughters of Canaan.' ... Jacob obeyed his father and his mother and was gone to Paddan-aram." (Genesis 28:6-9) The prevailing corrupt theology during the lifetime of the biblical patriarchs seems to have emanated and been sustained by teachers sent out from great centers like Choga Zanbil.

A ziggurat is the characteristic Mesopotamian tomb-temple built and dedicated to honor some deity. In this case the ziggurat was built by the Elamite King Untash Gal at about 1250 B.C. as a center of worship to Inshushinak, the chief god of Susa. The form of this ziggurat, and we understand it was basically the same for all, had five concentric square platforms on top of one another, the upper ones smaller than the ones below. In this case, the foundations of the upper platforms were carried to the ground and did not rest on the lower platforms!

The "tower" of Genesis 11:4 may well have been in the form of a ziggurat. The ziggurat of Choga Zanbil was 173 feet high. The top platform was about 86 feet square, while the bottom one was about 345 feet square. The most sacred area was at the extreme top, but many rooms and sacred areas were also in the lower terraces. All the terraces were connected by a rather complicated system of stairs. This temple structure was the center of a large religious city, Dur-Untash. The city was never fully completed because it was destroyed by the Assyrian King Ashurbanipal in about 640 B.C.

Chapter 12~World Capitals: Letter No. 8-B

Today there are high sand dunes between the Dez River and Choga Zanbil, but we are of the opinion that the sand dunes were not there in ancient times, and that in those days the ziggurat could have been seen for miles on the flat fertile plains of Susa, perhaps even from Susa itself.

The Susa Plains and the Dez River as seen from Choga Zanbil

The plains of Susa have been called "the breadbaskets" of the Achaemenian Empire. They may well become the breadbasket of modern Iran also. That potential is seen by the vast sugar cane plantations which dominate for miles around Susa. For example, on the road from Susa to Choga Zanbil, there is a modern cane-sugar mill, mated with a paper mill, which utilizes the stalks after extraction of the sugar. The water for this very modern agricultural scheme comes from the Dez Dam, an arched dam built between 1959 and 1963 under the rule of Mohammad Reza Pahlavi, the last Shah of Iran, located in the southwestern province of Khuzistan, Iran.

Also, about 10 miles from Susa on the road to Choga Zanbil is what some scholars think was the center of a splinter religious group in those days when Choga Zanbil was the main center. It is called Haft Tepe and the religious rites there seem to have involved human sacrifice. It is, perhaps, that point which caused the rift in ancient Elamite religion.

Though we are many miles now from Pasargadae and Persepolis, what I want to share with you does not break the continuity of our route. Perhaps it will even make it more clear. By the time we had arrived at Pasargadae, one of the things that had indelibly impressed itself on our minds was what great administrators Cyrus, Darius and Xerxes had been. Our whole trip has so far fallen in the domain of the Achaemenid Empire. (As noted before, the Empire is called Achaemenid after an ancestor of Cyrus the founder, King Achaemenus. Achaemenian is not only what others have called them but also what they called themselves. For example, on the stone corner column in Cyrus' private palace in Pasargadae is still clearly incised in cuneiform, "I, Cyrus, the King, an Achaemenian.")

The book of Esther reminds us how extensive the Achaemenian Empire was: "This is Ahasuerus who reigned from India even unto Ethiopia, over a hundred and seven and twenty provinces." (Esther 1:1) Well, we began this exploratory trip from Lahore, now in Pakistan, but in Achaemenian days considered part of the province of India. (I do not intend to imply that the city of Lahore, as such, existed in the days of the Achaemenian kings, but only that the site lay within the province of India. Still, Lahore is an ancient city and there may have been some settlement on the site in the days of Cyrus, but the first literary mention of the city seems to be about 800 A.D.)

You will recall that Alexander the Great was trying to subdue the whole Achaemenid Empire. To do so he conquered all the way to the Beas River (a tributary to the Indus River) located in what is now Pakistan. So, then, we started our trip from near the eastern limit of the Achaemenid Empire. We came close to the northern border when we reached the Amu Darya (Amu River), north of Kunduz. We have traveled for days and days just to reach the capital and we won't be out of the confines of the Empire till we reach Greece! We drive between forty and sixty miles per hour where road conditions permit. We cover in an hour what the Achaemenids covered in a day! An incident from the life of Henry Martyn, the great Bible translator, makes the contrast vivid. In May of 1812, having completed his translation of the New Testament into Persian, he set out from Shiraz to Tabriz to give it to the British Ambassador who would formally present it to the Shah. "Twelve days' hard riding brought him to Isfahan."[6] We drove the same distance in one long day and took out about three hours to examine the ruins of Pasargadae! Still, the Achaemenids superbly administered their vast and complex territory. We stand in awe of their competence and ability!

Of course, even in ancient times there were faster means of travel to which Achaemenid Imperial Administrators doubtless had access. A modern Irani cameleer claims a good riding camel can travel at a ten-mile-an-hour clip for 12 hours and repeat the performance after only a two hour rest.[7] Frederick Tallberg says that, "To ensure the control of development of his immense empire, Darius connected his cities by means of a network of ... roads, along which caravans could journey safely and comfortably, in the knowledge that at every twenty-four kilometers was a military post and a caravanserai. The swift post-riders on the famous 'Royal Road' covered a distance of 2,100 kilometers from Susa to Sardis in eleven days."[8] That works out to a daily average of 118.5 miles, which agrees closely with the cameleer's testimony. Still, the contrast with modern transport is striking and gives the Achaemenids very high marks.

Chapter 12~World Capitals: Letter No. 8-B

Now, at this point, another reality also may be easier to explain. When we arrived in Pasargadae we were at the capital of the Achaemenid Empire. When we went on to Persepolis, some 45 miles closer to Shiraz, we were also at the capital. Tonight we are in Susa and still, as the book of Esther makes unmistakably clear, we are at the capital. When we go on to Hamadan, the ancient Ecbatana, Achmetha in the Scripture (See Ezra 6:2.), we'll still be at the capital. The Achaemenid Empire was a multi-capitaled empire. First, when Cyrus the Great was ruling only Fars and Anshan (the southern half of Elam whose capital city was Susa), his capital was Pasargadae. When Cyrus conquered the Medes, whose capital was Ecbatana, and subdued their old empire, the Achaemenid Empire came into existence. During the life of Cyrus the Great, the founder and first emperor, the imperial capital continued to be Pasargadae.

Darius the Great, who succeeded from a different branch of the Achaemenians,[9] felt the capital at Pasargadae was not fitting for an empire stretching from the Indus River to the Aegean Sea. So he began the construction of Persepolis, the magnificent capital whose ruins after twenty-five centuries still awe and overwhelm one with their expanse, beauty and technical perfection.[10] But Pasargadae was not abandoned. Its three palaces, its Zoroastrian fire altars, the tomb of Cyrus and a mysterious building which well may have been the temporary tomb of Cambyses I, the father of Cyrus the Great, were all maintained in a splendid irrigated imperial garden. Paid magi were perpetually on duty to guard the tomb of Cyrus and offer the proper sacrifice in his honor. Whenever a new emperor was to be enthroned, he had to go to the tomb of Cyrus, enter a small room just below the gabled stone roof (the actual burial was in the gable in stone coffins, his wife being buried beside him) containing a gold sarcophagus[11] which was sort of a cenotaph[12] in reverse, put on the robe of Cyrus and take a vow to maintain the empire with diligence and loyalty. While all this was splendidly maintained, the additional architecture Cyrus had planned for the great platform he had built was never erected.[13]

All other important imperial pageantry and protocol was carried out in Persepolis. For example, it was there that the emperor celebrated the most important yearly festival, Nau Roz, (New Year's Day) every March at the Spring Equinox.

Here also the emperor celebrated the intercalary days, those days that had to be added to keep their lunar calendar from getting too far out of step with the solar year. Also, as a rule, all foreign ambassadors and dignitaries were received and entertained at Persepolis. Any emissary waiting in the anteroom, called The Gate of All Nations, for his audience with the emperor would simply have been overwhelmed with the grandeur and magnificence of that part of the vast palace complex he would already have seen. The magnificence yet to be beheld in the hall of audience would simply stun him with a sense of majesty. Probably any thought of disagreement with a royal suggestion would have been impossible.

Heartland of the Middle East

Susa had been the Elamite capital for centuries and it was chosen to be the administrative capital of the Empire. It was certainly more centrally situated than Persepolis. Also, it was warmer, being at a low elevation near the Persian Gulf. So, it was the winter residence of the emperors as well as the major administrative center. The famous Code of Hammurabi, king of Babylon, had been carried to Susa as booty by the Elamites. It remained there during all the Persian rule and finally was recovered during excavations at the site.

Allow me to digress for a moment. Perhaps after my description in a previous letter of the fine Iranian roads in Khorasan Province you'd like another report. Well, if you drive, as we did, from Persepolis, via Shiraz to Ahwaz and on to Susa, be prepared for many miles of very rough, unpaved roads with no road signs whatsoever. Darius did put in a good road with bridges, but during the many intervening centuries most of it has been ruined. Now the Iranian Highway Department is working hard to get things in shape. Probably, after a year or two, that drive through the very rugged southern Zagros Mountains will be pleasant, instead of jolting and tiring as it is now.

By the way, even though there are no road signs on much of the very difficult road from Shiraz, it was fairly obvious when we had reached Khuzistan Province, in which Susa is located. The oil wells, the pipe lines and the processing plants which feed the vast Abadan refinery immediately began to dominate the scene wherever we looked. Countless billions of BTUs of energy are wasted as they burn off the excess gases at hundreds of huge gas jets at those installations. The first impression was that either we had reached the portal of Dante's Inferno or that Zoroastrian Fire Altars had been re-established on a vast scale! Interestingly, some think that Masjid-e-Soleyman, where the first successful Iranian oil well was drilled in 1908, was the site of an ancient fire temple whose fire was fed by natural gas!

Now, back to the question of the capitals of the Achaemenian Empire. Ecbatana had been the capital of the Empire of Media before its conquest and absorption into the Persian Empire by Cyrus. Situated at a 6,280 foot elevation, it was the highest of all the capitals. It was developed even further by the Achaemenians for their summer capital, where they, and afterwards Alexander the Great, escaped from the heat. As I've already remarked, the ancient *tells*, as the huge mounds of ruins are called which mark the sites of ancient cities, are favorite sites for contemporary dwellers in these places. In Susa, the small town is just on one side of the *tell*, but at Ecbatana, unfortunately, the thriving modern city of Hamadan is squarely on top of the site!

Finally, I should mention briefly the role of Babylon, the last of the Achaemenian capitals. The city was not destroyed by Cyrus, but rather restored and adorned. It had been neglected at the end of the rule of Babylonian kings. Babylon became the capital of the largest of all the Satrapies. It was called the Satrapy of Babylon and Across-the-River (i.e. on the west side of the Euphrates). So, the whole area

Chapter 12~World Capitals: Letter No. 8-B

from the Tigris to the Mediterranean was normally governed from Babylon. That one double satrapy was imperial in size all by itself! In Ezra 5:13, Cyrus, the founder and first Emperor of the Achaemenid Empire, is called, "king of Babylon." That he was, but he was also much more. The appellation is in no way a denial of his greater role. Since the captivity of the Jews had been the work of a king of Babylon it is clear from Ezra 5:17 and 6:1 that an imperial archive was maintained at Babylon. That was completely in harmony with the extremely important administrative responsibilities which were centered there. By the time Ezra wrote, the great Satrapy of Babylon and Across-the-River had been divided as part of the punishment to Babylon for an abortive rebellion. The western part, from the Euphrates west, became the Satrapy Beyond-the-River over which Tattenai was the Satrap during Ezra's ministry (cf. Ezra 5:6). It is extremely interesting that the record needed in Ezra's case was not found in Babylon, but a copy was found in Ecbatana (Ezra 6:1-2). It seems they had an inter-library loan system!

Having committed the capital offense of talking too long about capitols, we ask your pardon from Shushan the Palace.

With love,
Lee and Jonathan

P.S. Those who'd like to learn more about the architecture of Persepolis would enjoy Donald N. Wilber's Persepolis, the Archaeology of Parsa, Seat of the Persian King, (New York: Thomas Y. Crowell Company, 1969).

---

1   A.T. Olmstead, History of the Persian Empire (Chicago: The University of Chicago Press, 1948), p. 60.
2   The Empire is called Achaemenid after an ancestor of Cyrus the founder, King Achaemenus. "Achaemenian"is not only what others have called them but what they called themselves. For example, on the stone corner columns in Cyrus' private palace in Pasargadae is still clearly incised in cuneiform, "I, Cyrus, the King, an Achaemenian."
3   The name "Persepolis" is Greek and is composed of two elements "Pers" referring to the Persians and "polis" meaning city in Greek.
4   Farnaz Fassihi & Steven Lee Myers, *China, With $400 Billion Iran Deal, Could Deepen Influence in Mideast,* The New York Times, March 27, 2021, p A1.

   "The countries signed a sweeping pact on Saturday that calls for heavy Chinese investments in Iran over 25 years in exchange for oil—a step that could ease Iran's international isolation. China agreed to invest $400 billion in Iran over 25 years in exchange for a steady supply of oil to fuel its growing economy under a sweeping economic and security agreement signed on Saturday. The deal could deepen China's influence in the Middle East and undercut American efforts to keep Iran isolated. But it was not immediately clear how much of the agreement can be implemented while the U.S. dispute with Iran over its nuclear program remains unresolved."

5   James T. Areddy, *China is Creating Digital Currency, First for a Major Economy,* The Wall Street Journal, April 6, 2021, p. A1.
6   Robin E. Waterfield, Christians in Persia, (London: George Allen & Unwin Ltd., 1973), p. 93.
7   William Graves, "Iran Desert Miracle," National Geographic Magazine, Vol. 147, No. 1 (January 1975), p. 41.
8   Fredrick Tallberg, From Cyrus to Pahlavi A Picture Story of the Iranian Empire 2nd ed. (Shiraz: Pahlavi University, 1967), p. 19.
9   As an editorial addition to this letter a chart of the house of Achaemenes will no doubt help keep relation-

ships in the royal line clear:

```
                    Achaemenes
                        |
                      Teispes
                        |
Cyrus I                          Ariaramenes
Cambysis I                       Arsames
Cyrus II (The Great)             Hystaspes
Cambysis II                      Darius (Hystaspes, The Great)
```

10 An earlier reading note, not accessible to me when I wrote this letter, may be helpful to some of you, "Construction was begun by Darius and continued by Xerxes and Artazerxes III." – Donald N. Wilber, Iran: Past and Present, (Princeton: Princeton University Press, 1948), p. 24.
11 Stone coffin
12 A monument to someone buried elsewhere
13 Reference to an older note, not available as I wrote this letter, gives a fascinating perspective on the development of these platforms: "Excavation has revealed the existence in Urartu of fortified towns with a Cyclopean construction unknown to the inhabitants of the Mesopotamian plain." This was the inspirational source for the Persian platform-terrace building. – R. Ghirshman, Iran, (Baltimore: Penguin Books Ltd., 1954), p. 92.

Chapter 12~World Capitals: Letter No. 8-B

Dez River Addendum

Driving north from Ahwaz, roads may become quite confusing because of the interconnections of roads which had been created solely to facilitate construction of the amazing Dez River Dam,

We had been on Iran's roads so long that we were becoming anxious about our 30-day Iranian travel permits expiring before we could cross an international boundary to get them renewed. Winds from the west had become chilling, having picked up the extremely cold temperatures of the thick Iraqi snowfall, lying heavily on the ground. Visualizing any possible itinerary, we remembered the threatening refusal of the Iraqi government to allow us to travel in or through their biblically historic country. (See Chapter 14.)

The Dez River Dam shown here reminds viewers of the 1936 U.S.A. Hoover Dam.
~ Sharam Khorasanizdeh, Shutterstock,

Location and initial GWh capacity of selected centers (Source: Wikipedia 9/09/21)		
Facility	Capacity	Date Completed
Ethiopian High Dam	16,153 GWh	still under construction
North Nile Egyptian Aswan High Dam	10,042 GWh	1970
Hoover Dam, U.S.	3,300 GWh	1936
Dez River Dam, Iran	1,783 GWh	1963

Definition: A kilowatt-hour is a unit of electrical energy equal to 1 kilowatt of power sustained for one hour. A gigawatt hour (GWh) = 1 billion watt hours and is equivalent to 1 million kilowatt hours.

Map of the Dez River Dam Area

Chapter 13

Background: Turkey

During our travel in Turkey, life was dominated by Turkish language everywhere. Rapid review may be helpful.

To visualize Turkey geographically, think of a rectangle lying on one side. Its long **northern** side is entirely defined by the Black Sea. The **southern** side is defined by the northeast shore of the Mediterranean Sea, with that alignment being carried all the way east to the Iranian border, which, along with the Armenian border to the north, forms the **eastern** boundary of the rectangle. The **western** boundary is mainly defined by the Aegean Sea.

Turkey connects the Black Sea with the Mediterranean by three related water channels: (1) water flowing to the Sea of Marmara through the Bosporus, (2) the Sea of Marmara, and (3) the Dardanelles Strait. That combined waterway allows water from the Black Sea to help compensate for the extreme evaporation from the Mediterranean Sea. The other main routes through which the Mediterranean receives water are the Strait of Gibraltar and the Nile River.

Geographically, Turkey is a transition area. It anchors on Asia but is separated from Europe only by the Aegean Sea. On the northwest, Turkey breeches the line of the Bosporus, the Sea of Marmara, and the Dardanelles to encroach upon Europe itself. Well then, it makes one wonder: is Turkey to be considered European or Asian, or both?

Just as Turkey's geography is ambivalent, so have been its politics and its culture. It has at different times looked both "east" and "west," an ambivalence which has gone on for centuries. Turkey was Asian while the Achaemenian Persians ruled it. It was forced to do an about-face when the Greeks under Alexander conquered it. However, Seleucus Nicator, Alexander's successor in this area, turned it "east" again. But the Romans then conquered it and turned it to the "west." That lasted through the Roman and Byzantine periods until the Turks, first the Seljuks and later the Ottomans, turned it to the "east" yet again. During the Ottoman period, obviously its predominant cultural alliance was with Asia and North Africa, that is, with the preponderance of Dar-ul-Islam, the Muslim world.

World War I brought another wrenching change in Turkey's cultural allegiance. This statement not only refers to her disastrous military alliance with Germany in that convulsive conflict, but especially to iron-willed, ruthless Kemal Ataturk's decision to point his attenuated and re-created country to the West. That broke the predominantly Asian allegiance which it previously had. To do this, Ataturk severed many long-standing ties to traditional Islam. He permanently dissolved the institution of the caliphate. Turkey was, from that point on, no longer the leader of the Muslim world. He made Turkish the national language. That doomed Arabic, the Islamic language par-excellence, to a minor role in Turkey, becoming only a very restricted clerical language. The newly emphasized Turkish language was to be written with a Roman or English alphabet rather than Arabic. Turkish men were forced to abandon the *fez* for Western hats. The brimless *fez* was ideal for the prostration inherent in Muslim prayer. With no brim, the Muslim men, who pray with covered heads, could put their heads on the ground, pointed toward Mecca, without removing their hats. Thus, the *fez* served both as a hat and a head covering for prayer. This enforced change in male wardrobe was a blow to mosque ceremony, further weakening Turkey's tie to Islam.

It should be carefully noted, however, that while Ataturk, "paying the West the homage of acknowledging its superior advancement, he did this in revolt against Western control."[1] His success was crowned by having the humiliating, World War I, Treaty of Sevres abrogated as far as Turkey was concerned and replaced by the congenial Treaty of Lausanne in 1923. The change in treaties became possible by Turkish forces driving Greeks out of the eastern Aegean lowlands.

Now, once again, Turkey seems to be changing its stance. It is becoming more and more disenchanted with its western ties and its western allegiance. It is turning to the Muslim East. Revived Islam is becoming dominant again in Turkey. Ties to the Muslim world are being revived and strengthened. This may well cause Turkey to forge intimate relations with its eastern Muslim Turkic cousins now occupying the old homeland of the Seljuks and Ottomans before their migrations to Anatolia[2] occurred. Should this develop much further, it could make Turkey even more vulnerable to domination by the Soviet Union. This raises the whole question of whether Turkey could work closely and compatibly with a Communist Russia. The answer may come from Turkey's earlier encounters with Communism.

One major reason Communism failed to make significant progress in Turkey during the time of Ataturk was the association of some of its factions with minority elements in the Turkish population. This was especially true of those Communist groups which enrolled a high proportion of Greeks in their rank-and-file. Such a group was the "International Union of Workers" in Istanbul, founded in 1920 under the leadership of Serafim Maximos. Such groups were especially odious to Turks since Greece had landed an expeditionary force at Izmir in 1919 and tried to conquer the major part of Anatolia.[3] Keeping the long history of Turkish-Greek animosity in mind, "it was, of course, quite unrealistic to expect to bridge the gulf between Greek and Turk during these war years."[4]

Another reason Communism failed to gain a significant foothold in Turkey was the pro-Russian stance of some of its factions. For example, the Turkish Communist Party, under the leadership of Mustafa Subhi, was based in Baku on the Caspian Sea in the Soviet Socialist Republic of Azerbaidzhan/Azerbaijan. This party not only "issued a strong declaration condemning the deceit of the Kemalists"[5] but tried to sow discontent among Russian refugees fleeing into Turkey

Chapter 13~Background: Turkey

from Soviet brutality as well as among Turkish prisoners of war returning from the Soviet Union into Turkey.

There was a third and very powerful reason Communism did not succeed in Turkey during the days of Kemal Ataturk. Ataturk was apparently astute enough to discern that the ferment in Turkey was clearly motivated by nationalist feelings, while Communism was, in theory at least, based on class consideration which transcended and, therefore, negated nationalism. Thus it was a moment in history where Turks generally were challenged far more readily and deeply by "Turkey for the Turks" than they could have been by the cry of "The dictatorship of the proletariat" or by "Workers unite!" In sum, "the First World War stimulated the development of Turkish national consciousness."[6] Ataturk seized upon the dominant popular mood and squelched everything else. At the same time he was adroit enough not to crush the mishmash of Communist groups so hastily that he would have antagonized the Soviets and lost the sorely needed economic and material assistance being given.

However, it should be clearly noted that it was neither antipathy to the Communist concept itself nor any consistently felt or perceived incompatibility between Communism and Islam which saved the Turkish revolution from a Communist destiny. In fact, "with the start of the Turkish struggle for independence, many Turks felt a certain kinship between their revolution and that of their Bolshevik neighbors. Not only did the Turkish intelligentsia tend to regard the experiment in Russia with friendly sympathy rather than alarm, but even extreme Turkish nationalists were inclined to believe that Soviet experience might have lessons applicable in Turkey. On the popular level, it was widely assumed that Communism was merely a re-statement of Islam, emphasizing the injunction to share ones' goods with the poor."[7]

"No longer envisioning a future in the West, Turkey is now more decidedly embracing its Islamic past, looking past lines and borders drawn a century ago. Its claim to the influence it had in the onetime domains of the Ottoman Empire can no longer be dismissed as rhetoric. Turkish ambition is now a force to be reckoned with."[8]

Turkey's disenchantment with its Western allies, especially with the United States, stems from the United States' stance on the Cyprus issue following the Turkish intervention there in 1974. The population of Cyprus is divided between the Greeks in the south and the Turks in the north. The Greek bishop Makarios decided to unify the island by subjugating the Turkish area. To protect her besieged compatriots Turkey launched an amphibious invasion force which soundly defeated the Greeks. The cease-fire line was more disadvantageous to the Greeks than the border had been before they began hostilities. Unfortunately, the Turks used military equipment obtained from the United States of America which, by treaty rights, could only be used to protect mainland Turkey from Communist aggression. §

1. Rene Albrecht-Carrie, The Meaning of the First World War, (Englewood Cliffs: Prentice-Hall, Inc., 1965), p. 163.
2. "The region is bounded by the Turkish Straits to the northwest, the Black Sea to the north, the Armenian Highlands to the east, the Mediterranean Sea to the south, and the Aegean Sea to the west." – https://en.wikipedia.org/wiki/Anatolia (Accessed 10/12/21.)
3. "The city and district of Izmir contained an important Greek population, and already in February 1919 Venizelos, the Greek Prime Minister, had presented a formal claim to them at the Peace Conference in Paris. The Italians, too, had a claim to Izmir, based on the superseded treaty of St. Jean de Maurienne, and it was largely in order to forestall the Italians that the allies agreed to a Greek landing. On May 1919, protected by British, French, and American warships, a Greek army landed at Izmir; after systematically occupying the towns and surrounding district, they began to advance eastwards into the interior. The Greeks made it clear from the first that they had come, not for a temporary occupation, but for a permanent annexation–to incorporate western Anatolia in a greater Greece on both shores of the Aegean, and thus bring nearer the 'Great Idea'–the restoration of the departed glories of the Greek Christian Empire of Constantinople." – Bernard Lewis, The Emergence of Modern Turkey, (New York: Oxford University Press, 1961), pp. 236-237.
4. George S. Harris, The Origins of Communism in Turkey, (Stanford: The Hoover Institution on War, Revolution and Peace, 1967), p. 102.
5. George S. Harris, The Origins of Communism in Turkey, (Stanford: The Hoover Institution on War, Revolution and Peace, 1967), p. 61.
6. George S. Harris, The Origins of Communism in Turkey, (Stanford: The Hoover Institution on War, Revolution and Peace, 1967), p. 31.
7. George S. Harris, The Origins of Communism in Turkey, (Stanford: The Hoover Institution on War, Revolution and Peace, 1967), p. 67.
8. Valt Nasr, *The Arab Moment Has Passed,* Foreign Policy, Spring 2021, p. 17.

Chapter 14

Esther & Mordecai

> Homeward-Bound Letter No. 9
> Erzincan, Turkey
> December 14, 1975

Dear Friends,

This is a clear Sunday morning. As the date line indicates, we are in Erzincan (pronounced "Erzinjan"), Turkey. We have, in fact, already spent two nights here. One remarkable thing about the situation is that we had never intended to stay in this area at all. Having arrived in this likable small town we would have moved right on except we needed a part for our Jeep's electrical system. This is the nearest town of any practical size near the place where the trouble began. But, as in so many previous places during our trip, shops were closed because of an Islamic religious holiday. This time it was the Muslim Eid-us-Zoha. So, we're trying to redeem the time by reading and writing till we can get on the road again.

Usually, if one looks for them, there may be blessings in altered plans. So it has been here. Without the delay we would have sallied right out of this place without time to have realized how strategic it is. A range of mountains called Murit Dagi, looming a short distance to the north, is a three-way watershed. From the north side, one river, the Aras (the ancient Araxes), flows east into the Caspian Sea and another, the Coruh, flows into the Black Sea. On the south side of the same mountains, in the same valley in which Erzincan is situated, begins the northern arm of the Euphrates River, "known as Karasu (Black Water)."[1] Also, this town, during the Seljuk and Mongol historic periods, according to Mango, was the most populous Armenian town in Turkey. There must have been many church buildings in those days. The reason none of the old church buildings remain (in addition to the shocking and stunning massacre of the Armenians by the Turks) is that the town was leveled in 1939 by a disastrous earthquake.

According to our original itinerary, after visiting Susa we would have crossed into Iraq to visit the great postdiluvian and early Patriarchal historical sites. Next, following the Euphrates, we would have entered Syria, where we hoped to visit Mari and Dura-Europos. From there we had wanted to make a straight course to Palmyra and Homs and then proceed south to Damascus and Jordan. The return from Jordan would have taken us through Syria into Turkey, where we wanted to visit a few of the sites of cities in which the apostle Paul had ministered. From thence we would have gone through Greece and Europe and so to America. At the moment, we are badly off that course because, first of all, the Iraqi government formally refused to grant us visas when we applied in Pakistan. However, we had hoped to have that unfriendly gesture reversed either in Kabul or Tehran. In

Kabul, the U.S. Counselor officer indicated that relations at that particular diplomatic post were so abysmally poor between the U.S. and Iraq that applying would almost certainly be an exercise in futility.2 Additionally, in Tehran, the Iraqi Embassy required a forty-day waiting period before they would tell anyone whether his application had been granted. We had neither time nor money for that experiment.

At that point, we made the first major change in our routing. Instead of visiting Hamadan and Kirmanshah on the way south from Tehran to Shiraz, we drove straight to Shiraz via Qum from Tehran, visiting Isfahan and Pasargadae en route. Shiraz was the base from which we explored Persepolis and Naqsh-e-Rustam, as the Achaemenid Royal Tomb area is called.

From Shiraz, our course was northwest to Ahwaz and then north to Susa, all mentioned in some detail in our earlier letters. Following our reversed itinerary we visited Hamadan and Kirmanshah on the way north from Susa.

In Hamadan, though we could not visit the ancient city of Achmetha (Ezra 6:2) since, as we mentioned in our last letter, it is squarely below the modern city and could not be excavated, we did visit the tomb venerated and protected by the local Jewish community as the tomb of Esther and Mordecai. However, their veneration may be misplaced in this instance. Esther, being the chief queen, was probably buried beside her husband the Emperor Ahasuerus (probably to be identified with Xerxes) in the royal tombs at Naqsh-e-Rustam, about six miles from Persepolis.

The royal tombs at Naqsh-e-Rustam, about six miles from Persepolis.

Chapter 14~Esther & Mordecai: Letter No. 9

However, Wilber sounds a word of caution about those royal tombs. "Only that of Darius bears inscriptions that name this ruler so that the assignment of the other tombs to later rulers represents merely informed speculation."[3] That seems to leave room for the Jewish community in Hamadan to be right after all.

In any case, it was a very rewarding experience to visit the tomb. There was more than a foot of snow covering the long path from the keeper's home to the tomb door. The wife of the keeper was embarrassed that the walk had not been shoveled and that she didn't have the key. Requesting us to return in half an hour she promised she would make the visit possible. Half an hour later, her seventeen year-old son, home from school, became our guide. The three of us, i.e. the keeper's son, Jonathan, and myself, shoveled the snow turn-by-turn right up to the door of the tomb. We were happily surprised to find that the tomb had a stone door. I had read of such doors still being used in large numbers in Jordan. We had seen that such doors had been used in the Royal Tombs at Persepolis and Naqsh-e-Rustam, but those had all been destroyed by tomb robbers. So, it was thrilling to me to see a stone door in actual use. This particular door was about four feet high (all who enter will of necessity bow in respect), about two-and-a-half feet wide and some seven inches thick. The great stone pivot pins which fit into stone sockets, top and bottom, were one piece with the door slab. In the door was a hole some six inches in diameter through which the keeper's son put one arm to unlock the sliding iron bar which held the door shut from inside. Surprisingly, the door turned noiselessly on its pivots. The lower pivot showed signs of having been greased.

The endless variety of doors which consisted of a stone slab may be grasped by viewing some doors in the collection here at the Damascus Museum.

Heartland of the Middle East

The tomb was divided into three rooms. The first was a small hall about 17 x 35 feet. Here, on the Feast of Purim (Esther 9:20-28), members of the local Jewish community assemble to commemorate God's deliverance of their ancestors. They do this very appropriately if, indeed, this is the tomb they consider it to be. From this hall a door led into the cenotaph chamber proper, a cubical room about 17 x 17 feet. The actual burial was in an underground stone chamber. The ceiling of that chamber is the floor on which the two carved ebony cenotaphs stand. Between the cenotaphs is a stone manhole cover with view ports in it through which one can see into the underground grave chamber in which an electric light is kept burning. Off the cubical cenotaph room is another cubical room where, in a special cupboard in one wall, the Jewish community of Hamadan preserves its oldest scroll of The Law. It is beautifully written on thick but soft leather. It was our privilege to examine and photograph it.

The only hotel which still had accommodation to offer that night in Hamadan was priced outside the maximum we were willing to pay. Despite continuing snow and biting, cold wind we determined we'd sleep in the Jeep just outside Hamadan, alongside the road to Kirmanshah, but close enough to walk back if we should get snowbound during the night. With four-wheel drive and tire chains we felt reasonably confident.

The road conditions on our way to Kirmanshah (pictured on the cover of this book).

Chapter 14~Esther & Mordecai: Letter No. 9

While our thoughts are still on Hamadan, you might be interested, as we were, to know that toward the end of the nineteenth century a significant number of the local Jewish community accepted Christ. We are indebted to Robin E. Waterfield for this insight. In brief, he says, "Thanks to the extensive itineration of such men as Stern, Bruhl and Sternschuss, Christian literature had been widely disseminated in Persia and eagerly accepted by Jews and Muslims. One of the most remarkable results of this work was the spontaneous formation of a little group of Jewish-Christian believers in the town of Hamadan. For the most part they were young men of well-to-do Jewish families, known and respected in the town. In 1878 four of them were baptized by the American missionary, James Bassett, then stationed in Tehran. Those baptized were Hezkiel Haym, Dr. Rahamin, Dr. Moosa and Dr. Aga Jan. Two years later their numbers had risen to forty men and fifteen women and they were suffering great persecution at the hands of the Jewish hierarchy, who even took the desperate step of handing over the converts to the governor, asking that they should be bastinadoed until they recanted. This, as well as imprisonment, payment of heavy fines to secure release and banning of all Jews from attending Christian places of worship, caused those fifty-five Christians to appeal to the CMJ in London; the message was relayed by Dr. Bruce. As a result, Joseph Letka, a Jewish convert from Lemberg and a missionary of some years' experience, was sent for a three-year tour to Hamadan to see what could be done to sustain and encourage the little Hebrew-Christian community."[4]

British orientalist Henry Creswick Rawlinson, scaling this cliff to the two-hundred foot level, transcribed the trilingual inscription for the first time.

Heartland of the Middle East

West of Hamadan, on the way to Kirmanshah, one of the passes was snowy and treacherous. Scores of trucks of an Iranian army convoy were stalled at various places up and down the pass waiting for more favorable circumstances. We were thankful to zigzag our way through without difficulty. Approximately 30 miles before Kirmanshah, at Behistun, on a sheer rock cliff, Darius the Great had carved in three languages (Old Persian, Neo Elamite and Neo Babylonian) in cuneiform script an account of his triumph over the usurper Gaumata.

The road in ancient times, as it does today, and did through all the intervening centuries, goes right along the base of the cliff where there is a lovely spring-fed pond, an inviting stopping place in favorable weather. Darius' planners knew uncounted thousands would read of the royal exploits. In modern times it was the British orientalist Henry Creswick Rawlinson who, scaling the cliff to the two-hundred foot level, transcribed the trilingual inscription for the first time. History has richly been rewarded by his efforts.

As Henri-Paul Eydoux points out, "he [Rawlinson] eventually succeeded in deciphering it. ... It was now possible to interpret the mass of documents already accumulated by archaeologists. ... Thus the decipherment of cuneiform had for Mesopotamian archaeology an important comparable with Champollion's decipherment of Egyptian hieroglyphs."[5]

Taq-e-Bostan, Kirmanshah

When we visited the spot it was so bitterly cold and the chill factor of the wind so high we did our photography as quickly as possible and then popped back into our ice-covered Jeep for protection.

Chapter 14~Esther & Mordecai: Letter No. 9

At Kirmanshah we had a two-fold purpose: to photograph the Sassanian rock carvings, about which there is no space here to give a description, and to collect our mail from the general delivery section of the main post office. It proved to be much harder to find the post office than the Sassanian carvings, but at least equally rewarding. Jonathan and I found the most unpleasant aspect of our trip was our inability to keep close contact with Gerry, Joanna and our other loved ones. Uncertain itineraries and winter conditions have made it impossible to be precise about places and times where mail could be sent. We appreciate the efforts loved ones have made to keep in contact by their letters of encouragement.

From Kirmanshah our route was to Rezaiah on the west shore of Lake Uramiah (now called Rezaiah in honor of Reza Shah Pahlavi). The route goes through the Province of Kurdistan. It is well-named. The population is predominately Kurd. They wear a distinct style of clothing and speak their own language. We had two interesting visits with Kurds which gave us the impression that Kurds feel the recent setback in their attempt at autonomy in Iraq cannot be reversed in this generation. One wonders whether Britain would have done better to have granted them a homeland when she relinquished rule of Mesopotamia. There are some ten million Kurds but they have never been able to generate world recognition for their right to a national homeland.

Just before crossing the border from Iran into Turkey, the main brake line on the Jeep split, leaving us with no brakes! By divine providence, only a few blocks back, an automotive mechanic had kept his shop open late into the evening. He had exactly the long piece of main brake tubing we needed with which he successfully repaired our brake system. Leaving Iran, we were greeted with this early morning view of Mt. Ararat in Turkey, the widely presumed mountain on which Noah's ark came to rest. (See Genesis 8:4.)

Our revised itinerary called for us to go due west from Rezaiah through the southeast corner of Turkey and into Syria. However, before leaving we were informed the road was snowed in till next spring. Two Iranian travelers had frozen to death trying to get through the route and a British party had been forced to turn back. So we revised plans again, going to the northernmost route which runs from Tabriz to Erzurum, and on to Erzincan where we are today. The route is not susceptible to less snow, but it is the main road link and is therefore kept open when others are blocked by snow. After a nighttime clearance from the Iranian customs and police we slept in the Jeep till Turkish authorities began processing documents the next morning.

With a farewell to Iran and a hello to Turkey we must end this letter.

> May you experience
> God's blessing,
> Lee and Jonathan

---

1 Andrew Mango, Discovering Turkey, (New York: Hastings House, 1971), p. 254.
2 The belligerence of the Iraqi Embassy grew out of a serious incident which occurred prior to our leaving Pakistan. On one occasion, while I was in the central police office in Lahore to get permission to drive beyond the Lahore District, the police officer in charge, a personal friend of mine, surreptitiously handed me a folded note which said my phone had been tapped and I was under surveillance by the Pakistan government because I, allegedly, was working as a spy to harm Pakistan! I told that police officer, whose name was also Turner, a heritage from his Anglo-Indian parentage, that I would contact him as soon as I had returned from my trip outside Lahore District. On my return, I took Officer Turner to our recording studio and offices to show him everything we were doing. I thought it was wise to make it clear to the Pakistani police that I was doing nothing subversively or surreptitiously.

   Later, I learned that the charge against me had been made by a disgruntled Pakistani member of the Shah Jamal Church because I would not agree to his desire to be appointed to a significant place of leadership in that congregation.

   When I applied to the Iraqi Embassy in Islamabad for a visa to visit Iraq on our trip through the Middle East, I received a very brusque, discourteous, flat refusal. I then contacted the American Embassy in Islamabad to see if they could encourage the Iraqi Embassy to grant my travel-visa application. The officer in the American Embassy also received a curt, almost insulting, refusal to consider their request which they had made on my behalf.

   There was a dormant ruling which had previously been issued by the Pakistani Government to all foreign embassies to clear all applications from foreign nationals for travel visas within Iraq with the Pakistani Government. Normally, being a very low profile request from Pakistan, that ruling was usually ignored by other countries' embassies in Islamabad.

   Earlier, while heavy pouches, shipped as "diplomatic mail" addressed to the Iraqi Embassy in Pakistan, were being unloaded at the Karachi Airport, one pouch accidentally fell from the cargo door of the plane. When it hit the concrete runway it broke open to disclose carefully packed military assault rifles, instead of normal embassy mail! Through that incident, Iraq had shown that it had been surreptitiously assisting anti-Pakistani revolutionary groups within the country! That development nearly caused a break of diplomatic relations between Iraq and Pakistan. Subsequently, Iraq was trying to make amends by submitting every visa application for approval by Pakistani authorities. Understandably, because of the completely false charge against me that I had been secretly trying to subvert Pakistani governmental authority, the Iraqi Embassy, which had learned of the accusation against me, was trying desperately to placate Pakistan and totally refused my request to visit their country.
3 Donald N. Wilber, Persepolis, the Achaeology of Parsa, Seat of the Persian Kings, (New York: Thomas Y. Crowell Co., 1969), p. 175.
4 Robin E. Waterfield, Christians in Persia, (London: George Allen & Unwin Ltd., 1973), p. 116.
5 Henri-Paul Eydoux, In Search of Lost Worlds, (London: Elek Books, 1962), p. 60.

Chapter 15

In Abraham's Steps

Homeward-Bound Letter No. 10
Aleppo, Syria
December 21, 1975

Dear Friends,

The night of December 16th we slept in the Jeep along the rain-swept road just a short way west of Diyarbakir, Turkey. Next morning, just a few miles west of that night's halting place, the road reached an elevation of nearly 4,000 feet. The rain turned to snow and vehicles were in difficulty, stopping right in the road to put on chains. We felt we probably could get through, relying on four-wheel drive, without chaining up. How grateful we were to successfully weave our way up through the stalled traffic. Only a short way past the summit we dropped below snowline and into rain again. Not far ahead, in rolling grazing land, we passed two inoperative American installations, both heavily guarded by Turkish troops. One appeared to be a satellite-tracking facility and the other some kind of "big ears" pointed toward Gog and Magog. The road continued to lose elevation and soon we were out of the inclement weather and enjoying the most gloriously sunny day we'd experienced for weeks! As mile upon mile of undulating natural pastureland fell behind, and more stretched ahead, as far as we could see, my thoughts turned more and more to the man whose presence there so many centuries earlier made Haran the goal of the present leg of our journey. I'd felt for a long time that Abraham had had a crisis at Haran, and the awesomeness of this vast expanse of verdant grazing land to the north of it accentuated my feelings.

Heartland of the Middle East

God's leading just hadn't gone beyond Haran, so Abraham had stayed there till there should be additional guidance. He had been sure God had brought him that far. Had he gone on, he would have been leaning only on his own understanding, but Abraham never intended to do that. Still, he knew God's call had not been completely fulfilled by the trek from Ur to Haran. The call had been very specific: (1) "Get thee out of thy land and (2) from thy kindred and (3) come into the land I will show thee." (Acts 7:3) Unfortunately, his father Terah, appropriating the leadership unto himself (Genesis 11:31), took the whole family, with Abraham, as far as Haran. Terah, perhaps, might have been quite happy in Haran. It was a great center of the moon worship to which he had been addicted in Ur. (Joshua 24:2) A great temple also helped make Haran one of the most important trade centers in all upper Mesopotamia. This fact is in harmony with the name Haran which means "route." Indeed, it was situated on one of the great trade routes of antiquity. But, above all, the pasture lands which stretched in all directions—far beyond one's range of vision—were ideal for the family's great flocks. Despite the many other flocks in the area, there would be no shortage of grass.

It may have been very appealing to Abraham to make permanent arrangements for his flocks somewhere near Haran. "After all," he may have been tempted to think, "how long can a man be expected to stay, as it were, in a state of suspension, in a situation where he is neither here nor there?" If "country" meant Ur, then he'd gotten out of it, but if it meant Mesopotamia, he hadn't. "God seems silent these days," he might have thought, "and no one can blame me for putting my own interpretation on the word 'country.'"

Looking east from Haran

As the many mounds of ruins testify, there were plenty of thriving towns in the vicinity of Haran. "Couldn't God's command to separate 'from thy kindred' be fulfilled," Satan may have suggested, "by settling near one of the other cities in the vicinity?" If at Haran, as Ellen Gunderson Trayler[1] suggests in her moving novel, <u>Song of Abraham</u>, Terah and Nahor both became believers and renounced

Chapter 15~In Abraham's Steps: Letter No. 10

idolatry, living in close proximity to his family, but still "from" them, could easily have been even more appealing to Abraham. Mrs. Trayler's conclusion about the conversion of Terah and Nahor seems to be based, in the case of Nahor, on Abraham's much later insistence that a wife for Isaac be sought only from Nahor's family, perhaps implying its members were also faithful to God. In Terah's case, all that may be suggested, so far as I am aware in favor of Mrs. Trayler's conclusion, is found in Genesis 15:15. This passage is a ringing affirmation of Abraham's salvation and that of the "fathers" to whom he was to "go" when he would be "buried in a good old age." But, was Terah necessarily among those "fathers?" Or, does it only refer to Abel, Enoch, Noah and others who had walked by faith (Hebrews 11:1-7) before Abraham and were, therefore, his "fathers"? While we all hope Terah is included, it seems there isn't enough evidence to be conclusive. Won't it be interesting to get the answer to that and similar obscurities when, before the throne, we join that great throng mentioned in Revelation 7:9-10?

The second call (Genesis 12:1-3) must have brought great relief and peace to Abraham, though even yet he was not saved from the ambiguity of his travels. His call was still only "unto the land I *will* show thee." (Genesis 12:1) One can never be saved from raised eyebrows when he can't be precise even about his own affairs. Thank God, Abraham was willing to endure, not only separation and ambiguity but a ridiculous position as well, for "he went out, not knowing whither he went." (Hebrews 11:8)

Our base for visiting Haran was Urfa, Turkey. Hitti points out that, "the earliest form of its name is Aramaic *Urhai*, which survived in Arabic *al-Ruha*, corrupted into Turkish *Urfa*."[2] To students of eastern church history, Urfa will be better known as Edessa. It was the earliest center of Christianity in Mesopotamia. The famous Diatessaron, the earliest harmony of the Gospels, and the Syriac translation of the Bible were both prepared here. One of the earliest kings known to have accepted Christ was King Abgar VIII of Edessa, on whose coins, minted between 180 and 192 A.D., he is shown with a cross on his headdress. There was a very influential seminary in Edessa which was probably founded (though it may only have been reorganized) by Ephraim Syrus in the fourth century.

We had a most unsatisfactory hotel situation in Urfa which discouraged us from staying more than one night in this one-time great center of Christianity. It continued to be a Christian center long after the area came under Muslim control. In this city, the first Umayyad Caliph, Mu'awiya, even restored a church building that had been destroyed by an earthquake. However, later Muslims completely uprooted all Christian institutions and today, ironically, there is not a single resident Christian in the city! Nevertheless, Jonathan and I both suspect remnants of church architecture would still be noticeable if one had time to leisurely stroll through its many narrow, winding streets. It is the most "Oriental" of any Turkish city we have visited so far on this trip.

Heartland of the Middle East

The site of Haran is today a *tell* (or mound) a short distance west of the River Balikh, not far south of Urfa. The two most notable archaeological remnants date far after Abraham's visit. One is the ruins of a building known to local inhabitants as a university, which it well may have been, for there was a famous Christian school here and, later, a Muslim school of medicine.

It is my impression, though I cannot give any reference for it, that Haran used to be situated right on the bank of the Balikh River at the time Abraham visited the city. If so, the river, as most do through the centuries, has changed course, moving far enough to the east that, today, one cannot see it clearly from the top of the mound of ruins. However, from the top of the Haran *tell* one can see many other *tells* dotting the upper Mesopotamian plain. I had read many times of this feature of Mesopotamia, but had never felt the full impact of it till standing on the mound of Haran. *Tells* loomed as far as we could see; silent, yet eloquent, witnesses to the antiquity and continuity of civilization in the Fertile Crescent.

Some impression of the vigor of moon worship and paganism in Haran can be gained from two glimpses of them many centuries after Abraham's temporary residence there. The last king of Babylon, Nabu-naid, was the son of the high priest of the moon temple at Haran. During the struggle between Media and Assyria for control of Haran, the moon-god temple had been destroyed. However, the high priest, Nabu-naid's father, continued to reside in the ruins. It was the desire of Nabu-naid to rebuild the temple for his father that caused him to ally Babylon with the Persians in the struggle against the Medes. Haran was soon wrested from the Medes and Nabu-naid rebuilt the temple. In doing so he neglected claims of the various priests of Babylon, thus alienating them from him and setting the stage for Babylon to be annexed shortly into the rising Persian Empire. Those Babylonian priests sneered at the new temple in Haran, saying that the king had "made an abomination, a no-sanctuary, and for it he made an image which he *called* Sin; it was not the familiar moon-god of Babylonia, but was like the moon in its eclipse."[3] Though the image showed the moon in eclipse, the worship of the moon in Haran did not go into eclipse nearly so soon as it did in Babylon, the home of the scoffers. Paganism was so resilient in Haran that it survived during the whole Christian period of the city's history, thus calling forth the odious appellation "the heathen city" in the writings of the Church Fathers. After the Christian period, "paganism survived the Muslim conquest and was not extirpated until the eleventh century."[4]

Abraham doubtless followed the Balikh River north from the Euphrates to reach Haran. However, what route he took from Haran to Palestine is conjectural. He may have retraced his steps along the Balikh to its junction with the Euphrates near the Syrian town of Raqqa. But it is equally possible that, as we did, he went west from Haran to Carchemish (the present Jarabulus on the north Syrian border and not Hamath as Mrs. Gunderson mistakenly asserts in her novel) and from there to Aleppo and Damascus.

Chapter 15~In Abraham's Steps: Letter No. 10

(We had tried to go down the Balikh into Syria. Though all our maps show a border crossing at Akcakale, Turkey, we found on arrival that it doesn't exist in fact.) We know Abraham went through Damascus, and from references to his chief servant Eliezer (Genesis 15:2-3), he probably tarried there for some time.

Carchemish is famous as the site of a battle between the forces of Egypt, under Pharaoh Neco (II Chronicles 35:20), and the neo-Babylonian army under Nebuchadnezzar in 605 B.C. Neco's forces were overwhelmingly defeated (Jeremiah 46:2). This settled the question whether the political history of the eastern Mediterranean, during the ensuing decades after the destruction of Assyrian power, would center on the Nile or on the Euphrates. The present small quiet town of Jarabulus, with its neat whitewashed box-like Syrian homes, hardly reminds one of the stirring and significant events which have taken place there.

The Citadel in Aleppo

On the basis of English news and weather forecasts from Radio Israel, we have decided to travel in eastern Syria before trying to visit the northwestern part of this country.

May we all walk in the steps of the faith of our father Abraham (Romans 4:12).

With love,
Lee and Jonathan

---

1   Ellen Gunderson Trayler, <u>Song of Abraham</u>, (Wheaton: Tyndale House Publishers, 1973).
2   Philip K. Hitti, <u>History of Syria</u>, (London: Macmillan & Co. Ltd., 1957), p. 253.
3   A.T. Olmstead, <u>History of the Persian Empire</u>, (Chicago: The University of Chicago Press, 1948), p. 54.
4   Andrew Mango, <u>Discovering Turkey</u>, (New York: Hastings House, 1971), p. 43.

A later note may be helpful. The moon symbol (the crescent, which was on the coinage of Marcus Aurelius and of Carocalla, minted in Haran) has survived in the crescents on the domes of the mosques throughout the Near East. (See H. J. W. Drijvers, <u>Cults and Beliefs at Edessa</u>, (Leiden: E.J. Brill, 1980), p. 202, plate xxx11.) During our trip, Jonathan and I frequently spoke of this prominent feature of the mosques. For anyone wishing a fuller discussion of moon worship at Haran, <u>Cults and Beliefs at Edessa</u>, is particularly helpful (especially pp. 141-145). The average reader will be well advised to borrow this book from some good library, since its American importer has set the price between $49 and $54 dollars, depending on how one purchases it! (Note: February 2021, lowest price found was $178.52!)

CHAPTER 16

THEY LOVED NOT THEIR LIFE

Homeward-Bound Letter No. 11
Ressafa, Syria
December 23, 1975

Dear Friends,

Tonight, December 23rd, Jonathan and I are bedded down in the back of our Jeep in the Syrian desert some one hundred miles east of Aleppo and some twenty miles south of the Euphrates River. We miss our family very much, especially since we haven't seen any of them since July 3rd and it is a traditional family get-together season. Except for this loneliness and desire to have the family together, we consider it a great blessing to be here. It is cold here in the desert. Our breath will condense on the windows and freeze our blankets to the glass by morning. As soon as the sun sets, freezing begins outside. Still, we think the experience is worth a lot of inconvenience.

We are in the desert, but we are also in a large city, though tonight we have it all to ourselves. This afternoon there were two local Arab shepherd girls here who sold us some old Roman, Greek, and Abbasid coins they had found in the city, but they left about three hours ago when the sun set and now the city is ours.

A cordial shepherd girl invited us to stay at Ressafa.

Nathan McCarty, who judges sheep in the Oregon State Fair and in county fairs, says, "I suspect the breed to be Awassi." "It is the dominant breed in Iraq, the most important sheep in the Syrian Arab Republic, and the only indigenous breed of sheep in Lebanon, Jordan and Israel." – www.FAO.org, quoting Pritchard, Pennell & Williams, 1975.

This city is mentioned in the Bible as Rezeph (II Kings 19:12, Isaiah 37:12). Much later it was a trading-outpost city under rule of Palmyra. All during Roman times it was on the sensitive eastern border facing the dangerous Parthian Empire. In the year 305 A.D., during the emperorship of Diocletian, a Roman border patrol was making its way south to Ressafa. Two Christian officers were in the detachment. About fifty miles to the north, at Meskenah, both these men were badly beaten by men of the patrol to induce them to abjure their faith in Christ. Both refused. Bacchus, one of the officers, died of the beating but Sergius, the other one, survived.

Here at Ressafa, Sergius was forced to run eighteen miles in shoes with nails which pierced his feet. He still refused to deny Christ and was then beheaded here to stop his heresy. Members of his detachment and citizens of the city were deeply touched by Sergius' resolute faith. Word of his martyrdom soon spread and Christians, to pay respect to his memory, began coming to Ressafa in great numbers. This eventually raised the city to its greatest glory.

A small church building, which no longer exists, was built over the burial place of Sergius as a place where his admirers could worship. The coming of pilgrims continued and their numbers became significant. Hostel and market facilities were needed to accommodate them. The city was renamed Sergiopolis to honor the most worthy man who had ever visited it.

To accommodate the hordes of pilgrims, one of the Roman emperors, probably Anastasius (491-518 A.D.), built a large basilica-type church building at the burial place of Sergius. The city, despite its vulnerable position on a sensitive and dangerous border and its inconvenient location at a great distance in the desert, experienced a period of rapid growth.

Later, because of the numbers who continued to arrive, the water supply of the city had to be supplemented. So Anastasius ordered vast underground cisterns to be carved from the bedrock of white quartz-like rock. These were roofed over with stone vaults. The workmanship was superb and the whole system is basically intact yet today. The Emperor Justinian had new fortifications built around the city, a mighty rampart of walls and towers with slots for bowmen, all interconnected by internal passages leading from tower to tower and from magazine to magazine around the entire perimeter.

The North Gate, used by Roman Legates.

Outside was an encircling moat. So well was the fortress designed that only one time were the defenses breached. The walls are largely intact but have suffered from war, earthquake and stone thieves using the place as a convenient quarry. Surprisingly, the ceremonial north gate, flanked by beautiful iconic columns capped by corniced arches, is wonderfully intact. One can easily visualize the visit of

Chapter 16~They Loved Not Their Life: Letter No. 11

a Roman Legate coming through the gate in imperial pomp with a fanfare of trumpets.

This beautiful church building at Ressafa resembles a Roman Basilica. The circular structure in the middle of the hall was where the church ministers sat to visit with congregants as they entered.

One of our main interests had centered on the ruins of the basilica, as the main meeting area in the church was commonly called in Roman times. We wanted to understand from the architectural details as much as possible about the faith and practice of the congregation. Unfortunately, time and predators have taken too high a toll for many points to be clear about which we would like to know. But, the beautiful marble Beema is still almost intact. That tells us this Christian basilica was Byzantine. The Beema was a place where the "Bishop" and the "clergy" sat in the center of the "nave," as the central section of the auditorium was called, during part of the worship service. On many pillar capitals, some fallen, others still in place, bas-relief crosses are still beautifully clear. Presumably, then, the church must have considered the sacrifice of Christ quite central. Also in the ruins are several bas-relief Alpha and Omega medallions (Revelation 1:8, 21:6, 22:13). From these, it seems their faith was firm in "the high and lofty One that inhabiteth eternity, whose name is Holy" (Isaiah 57:15).[1]

Tonight, more than any city plan or any kind of church architecture could possibly impress us, we are moved by the steadfast faith of Sergius and his companion Bacchus who "overcame him [the accuser of our brothers] because of the blood of the Lamb, and because of the word of their testimony; and they loved not their life even unto death" (Revelation 12:11).

Oh Father! May we all share fully in the victory of our Lord Jesus in whose name we appeal to thee. Amen.

> Good night with love,
> Lee and Jonathan

Current Event Note: While we visited Palmyra in complete safety, the site of the ancient city and the area surrounding it have become exceedingly dangerous. "Russia unleashed air strikes that it said killed as many as 200 militants in central Syria amid an intensifying assault by Islamic State insurgents that threaten the Syrian government's access to oil and heightens the risks for its foreign backers. The air strikes on a training camp took place Monday in Palmyra, according to Alexander Karpov, deputy chief of the Russian Center for Reconciliation of the Opposing Parties in Syria, a military entity." – Jared Malsin in Istanbul and Nazih Osseiran in Beirut, *The Wall Street Journal*, April 21, 2021, p. A18.

---

[1] A much earlier reading note to which I had no access while writing this letter from Ressafa may be of considerable interest to many readers. It tells of the observations of a Muslim traveler who visited Ressafa in the eleventh century A.D. "The Physician Ibn Butlan who wrote in 443 [A.H.] (1051) describes Rusafah as possessing a church, said to have been built by the Emperor Constantine, the exterior of which was ornamented in gold mosaic work and underneath was a crypt, as large as the church, with its roof supported on marble pillars. In the 5th (11th) century most of the inhabitants were still Christian, and they profitably combined brigandage with the convoying of caravans across the desert to Aleppo." – G. Le Strange, <u>The Lands of the Eastern Caliphate, Mesopotamia, Persia, and Central Asia from the Moslem Conquest to the Time of Timur,</u> (Cambridge: The University Press, 1905), p. 106.

CHAPTER 17

ENTREPOTS IN THE DESERT

Homeward-Bound Letter No. 12
Palmyra, Syria
December 27, 1975

Dear Friends,

After five nights of sleeping in the back of the Jeep, tonight we are "luxuriating" in a pre-Victorian hotel room in Palmyra, the capital of Queen Zenobia, ruler of the Palmyrians. Bible lovers will perhaps recognize the place more readily if I say we are luxuriating in Tadmor (II Chronicles 8:4).

In our last letter we mentioned that Ressafa (the Rezeph of II Kings 19:12) was a trading outpost of Palmyra. East of Ressafa it was our privilege to visit another one of those outposts, Dura-Europos. Great as Ressafa was, Dura was greater. Realizing they were only outposts of Palmyra should prepare one a bit for the magnificent ruins of this once great metropolis, or mother city.

In spite of its vast extent, Dura-Europos has yielded priceless treasures of past life and glory.

One of the problems inherent in excavating a city such as Dura-Europos is that buildings and paintings, exposed again to the elements after centuries, deteriorate rapidly unless special precautions are taken. The precaution that was taken in this case was to remove the most important items to museums. As a result, when one visits Dura the impact doesn't live up to the description, "the Pompeii of the East," which one writer used. Another problem about the ruins of Dura is, except for the city wall, it was not built of solid stone blocks, as Ressafa had been, but was either of rubble or, in many places, stone and mortar construction which deteriorates much faster than solid stone. It was a much larger city than Ressafa. For example, according to Hitti, the public square (called an agora) in the center on which the temples faced "was of 28,079 square yards."[1] Understandably, ruins of such magnitude could not all be preserved, but we felt one of the fortified gates, which are still in relatively good condition, could have been repaired and used as a site museum and perhaps one or two important buildings with some of the streets could have been preserved just to help visitors grasp its former glory.

One side of the city butted up against the right bank of the Euphrates River. The river bank here is high and perpendicular. The water literally boils past at this point. This side of the city needed little or no wall for safety, and the city was protected right and left by two deep ravines running into the Euphrates. On the remaining side, which could be approached without any natural barriers, a black basalt wall had been built, one of the most impressive city walls we've seen.

Though the wall was in precarious condition, we were able to drive through it without incident.

The site of the city was on the desert road connecting the capitals of Mesopotamia and Syria. It was established by Seleucus I, founder of the Seleucid Empire. When that empire faded it gave opportunity for Palmyra to flourish. Dura then came under its influence. Later, the Romans used it as a frontier post. It was finally

Chapter 17~Entrepots in the Desert: Letter No. 12

destroyed by the Sassanian Persians about 256 A.D. and was in the custody of the desert from that time till excavated in recent years.

Two of the excavated buildings were of special interest. One was a local church building, the oldest so far excavated anywhere. It was dated by the archaeologists at about 232 A.D. "From the inscriptions on its walls it appears that the congregation was Greek-speaking. Syriac, however, became the major medium for the spread of Christianity in the Tigris-Euphrates Valley."[2] We look forward to reading the archaeological reports (Yale University) to get a description of that building. The contrast with later church architecture should be marked and instructive. The other building was a third century synagogue whose interior had been decorated with murals depicting the great moments in the history of God's people. Those murals were taken to Damascus and installed in a replica synagogue in the National Museum. We anticipate seeing them.

Further east, just a short way west of the small town of Abu Kamal, are the ruins of the ancient Amorite city of Mari under excavation by the French since its discovery in 1933. The palace covered ten acres and was a complex of hundreds of rooms, which was completely excavated only after five seasons of dedicated labor. The city was destroyed by the armies of Hammurabi in the 18th century before Christ. However, nearly 4,000 years later, under the mound, the walls still stood to a height of fifteen feet. Professor Parrot, who did the initial digs, wrote, "the installations in the palace kitchens and bathrooms could still be put into commission without the need of any repair."[3]

There was a temple of Ishtar and one of Dagon, which was guarded by a bronze lion, now in the Aleppo Museum. We were surprised by the asphalted brick walkways we saw, which were still in excellent condition, as well as drainage systems that looked perfectly serviceable. The greatest reward, however, from the work at Mari was the recovery of more than 25,000 clay tablets from the palace archives. It will require many years of patient study before scholars will have completed the translation of that surfeit of documentary material. Already much has been learned. Haran, it is now known, was an Amorite city. "It is striking that towns in the area had (according to the Mari documents) names that in the Biblical tradition are credited to Abraham's relatives: Peleg, Serug, Nahor, Terah, Haran."[4] As James B. Pritchard says of the documents, "Personal names, language and customs reflect the culture of the Patriarchal Age in Genesis."[5] Much of the mud brick city has perished since its excavation but we are thankful for the significant bit we saw.

The seven miles (or so) on to Abu Kamal were quickly covered. After filling our regular tank, one auxiliary tank (the valve on the other one was not working properly), and a couple of G.I. cans with gasoline, we decided—since it was only about 3:00 p.m.—to start the long trek to the west across the desert to Palmyra.

A view of Mari where more than 25,000 clay tablets from its archives have been made available for study and research by competent, dedicated scholars.

Once one's course intersects the oil pipeline, coming from Iraq and on to the Syrian coast, he simply follows that mile-after-mile through the desert to Palmyra. Until one does reach the pipeline, unless he knows the maze of tracks well, it is entirely possible to inadvertently go south too quickly and cross into Iraq.

Those dear people, the Iraqis, are not known to be cordial to those who commit that error, so we were exercising special care with our navigation. That maze of tracks is caused by the Bedouins who go to and fro from their camps at either end of the route in Chevy pickups that make our old Jeep look awfully out of style. Except for the coming and going of the Bedouins at each end, one is entirely on his own over most of those 245 kilometers of desert. We had hoped to reach the pipeline before dark and stop there for the night. All went well till the sky suddenly filled with dense clouds which blotted out the evening light, making it impossible to tell which track was the main one. Several times we thought we had found the right way, only to be disappointed a short way ahead, when it went off in an erratic direction or faded out altogether. We made large sweeping circles, hoping the right track would show in our Jeep's lights. Again and again we came back to the same spot, a long stretch of mud which hadn't been crossed recently. The wind picked up, lightning began cleaving the sky and rain set in. We pulled to a high spot and bedded down. I prayed the temperature wouldn't drop and turn the rain to snow, nor that too much rain would fall, turning the dry ravines into raging torrents, impossible to ford.

Chapter 17~Entrepots in the Desert: Letter No. 12

Thankfully, the morning was clear. Through binoculars, a telephone line to our left could be seen which, according to our dime-store compass, was located where the pipeline presumably was. But, we hadn't known before that a telephone line was part of the installation. Anyway, we followed the track that took us to the phone line. Ironically, it went just beside the mud patch but had not been visible the night before. Again, consternation. The track crossed the pipeline and headed in the direction of Iraq. After consulting our maps again, we were certain there was enough distance for us to explore the track. Perhaps it would turn and come back to follow the north side of the pipe as our maps showed us it should. About four kilometers beyond the pipeline, that obstinate track turned right and headed north again. Shortly, we saw why it had taken such an erratic course. To cross a sizable ravine, it had to make a big swoop to get the right alignment. We were assured also by a cemented fording place in the bottom of the ravine, the only one on the whole stretch. We had found the way!

The only additional anxious moments till we reached Palmyra were those spent trying to pick the spots offering the least number of jagged rocks as the Jeep climbed in and out of ravines. We would have reached the Zenobia Hotel in time for supper, but our trailer tires were getting thin and we had to change them twice just on the outskirts of Tadmor. Our room here is too barn-like for the tiny heater to take the chill off, and the shower floods the bathroom, leaving water over an inch deep standing around the toilet, but we thank God we are safely here.

Palmyra is an oasis whose life had depended through the centuries on the generous flow of one sulphurous spring. The name Tadmor, though its meaning is not certain, is ancient. "There is a mention of it in an Assyrian contract dating from the beginning of the second millennium B.C., as well as in two letters discovered at Mari."[6] The city-state became an empire under the leadership of the widowed queen, Zenobia, who was not only as beautiful as Cleopatra, but also much more capable.

The kingdom was one of three pre-Islamic Arab states which rose on the periphery of the great Arabian Desert. The other two were the Nabataean and the Ghassanid. The kingdom of Palmyra first distinguished itself as an ally of Rome, protecting the eastern frontier. Its soldiers pushed all the way to Persepolis in a fruitless attempt to rescue the Roman Emperor Valerian, who had been captured by the Persians at Edessa. Later, Zenobia's armies carved an empire out of the eastern provinces of that same Roman Empire. The Emperor Aureliean finally restored those provinces to Rome, captured Zenobia, and took her to Rome where, in chains of gold, she was forced to walk in Aurelian's march of triumph!

Well, all that, thrilling as it is, takes me away from an important point I want to mention before closing. Almost any "up-to-date" commentary scoffs at II Chronicles 8:4, which tells us, "he (i.e. Solomon) built Tadmor in the wilderness."

I've only read one commentator who, as a word of caution, after reiterating the ridicule, reminds the reader that a full excavation has not been done and therefore, perhaps one should not yet be too dogmatic.

We were happy to see the very deep exploratory trenches in the courts of the temple of Baal. It is entirely possible, if that type of exploration is carried on, that epigraphic corroboration of II Chronicles will be discovered. We feel we can trust the scripture fully, even without the other evidence. That has been demonstrated innumerable times. About the word "built" in the passage, kindly note that it does not say "founded." For a similar use of the terminology, see Numbers 32:37-38.

The sense of civic coherence is captured in the remnants of structures like this amphitheater which was one of the focal points of civic life.

For the critics who scoff at the record in II Chronicles 8:4 (as well as at other passages), the words of Andrew Mango may prove prophetic: "The Iliad was proved to be a better guide than the theory that the Trojan war was but a version of a common European myth symbolizing the struggle between night and day and 'the victory of the solar hero around the walls and battlements of the sky.' Although in recent years the discovery of the Dead Sea Scrolls has similarly vindicated the Massoretic text of the Old Testament, the lesson has yet to be learned by the demythologisers."[7]

For a description of the magnificent ruins of Palmyra, as in the case of Persepolis, since adequate discussion is hardly possible in a letter of reasonable length, you might enjoy the two fine illustrated chapters in Henri Paul Eydoux's excellent

Chapter 17~Entrepots in the Desert: Letter No. 12

book, In Search of Lost Worlds: "The Exploration of Palmyra" and "The Great Phantoms of Palmyra."

The stunning ruins of Palmyra declared its centuries-long glorious predominance until they were recently deliberately destroyed by bestial Muslim raiders.

Hoping all of us are looking "for the city ... whose builder and maker is God" (Hebrews 11:10).

With love,
Lee and Jonathan

---

1 Philip K. Hitti, History of Syria, (London: Macmillan & Co. Ltd., 1957), p. 268.
2 Kenneth Scott Latourette, A History of Christianity, (New York: Harper & Row, Publishers, 1953), Vol. I, p. 79.
3 Werner Keller, The Bible as History, (New York: William Morrow & Co. 1956), p. 46.
4 Bernhard W. Anderson, The Living World of the Old Testament, (London: Longmans, Green & Co. Ltd., 1957), p. 23.
5 James B. Pritchard (ed.), The Ancient Near East, An Anthology of Texts and Pictures, (Princeton: Princeton University Press, 1958), p. 260.
6 Henri-Paul Eydoux, In Search of Lost Worlds, (London: Hamlyn, 1971), p. 261.
7 Andrew Mango, Discovering Turkey, (London: B.T. Batsford Ltd., 1971), p. 192.

Heartland of the Middle East

Chapter 18

East of Jordan & Aqaba

Homeward-Bound Letter No. 13
Karak, Jordan
January 16, 1976

Dear Friends,

Bashan, Gilead, Decapolis, Rabbath-Ammon, Moab, and Edom. What a flood of Biblical associations sweep before us with just the recital of that list of six names! I am penning these words from Karak in ancient Moab. We had hoped to spend the night on El Lisan, "The Tongue," as the peninsula jutting into the Dead Sea from the east shore is called. But we were turned back at a Jordanian army checkpoint because we did not have special permission from the provincial governor. So our Jeep had to climb the steep road carved on the south brim of the Wady Karak to the town of Karak, the "Kir" of Moab (Isaiah 15:1). We are lodged in the only public housing we could find. It is in the much too expensive Jordanian-Government-Hotel-and-Rest-House-Corporation's Crusader Castle of Crac des Moab. We had tried two places to camp along the road but were surprisingly refused permission. The Moabite tradition of hospitality seems to have deteriorated since the days of Elimelech and Naomi! (See the book of Ruth.)

The entire area from Bashan to Edom is dominated by three physical features: 1) The Ghor (as the Jordan River Canyon is called),[1] 2) the Anti-Lebanon Mountain Range (paralleling the Ghor on its east side, which later, south of the Dead Sea, is called the Arabah) running from Homs, Syria to the Gulf of Aqaba (often spelled Akaba), and 3) the Arabian Desert which marches the whole distance north to south, just on the eastern side of the mountains. East of the mountains, important centers of population have flourished only where adequate sources of water have been available. Otherwise, the loneliness of the desert has been broken only by the seasonal migration of the Bedouins.

Damascus, north of Bashan, is one of the few favored spots; though in the desert, it is nevertheless a verdant garden spot. Two rivers, the same two about which Naaman boasted (II Kings 5:12), the Barada (the biblical Abana) rising in the north and al-A'way (the biblical Pharpar) rising in the south on Mt. Hermon, make the existence of the flourishing city of Damascus possible. We followed the Barada up its shallow valley till we were near the border of Lebanon and then, because of the conflict raging just a short way ahead,[2] turned sadly back to Damascus. The river is divided into many branches as it nears the city and is used for irrigation. One area near the city, called al-Ghutah, has been a famous garden and orchard area for centuries. It is still verdant but threatened by encroaching roads and commercial construction.

This photo of Damascus powerfully augments the verbal picture in this letter. It shows many unfinished rooms occupied by desperate people who have only a sheet of plastic to give them privacy and protect them from sharp winds and raw temperatures. The demographic power of this historic city is captured by Lawrence of Arabia in the last two or three chapters of his gripping autobiography, <u>Seven Pillars of Wisdom</u>.

Damascus was the northernmost city of the Decapolis, as the league of [ten] Roman cities was called whose culture was Greek. However, today one senses none of the flavor of that ancient commercial and cultural league when one visits the throbbing capital of the Syrian Arab Republic. Driving in the city is only for those who know it well or for those, who, like me, have a first-class navigator [Jonathan] reading the inadequate city map and giving timely instructions about which lane to be in and which turn to take.

The National Museum in Damascus is outstanding, but a bit overwhelming because of the scope and wealth of its collections, encompassing every period from Mari (discussed in Letter No. 12) on one end, to the Umayyad Caliphate on the other. We particularly enjoyed the restored Jewish Synagogue from Dura-Europos (also mentioned in Letter No. 12). We marveled that specialists had been able to bring the plaster-wall murals and install them without damage in an exact replica of the Dura Synagogue. The murals, which originally covered every inch of the interior, were one way the Jewish community of Dura tried to keep the most important episodes of its national life vividly in memory. Thus, the artist's conception of Moses at the burning bush, the disaster of Pharaoh's army in the Red Sea, and other landmarks of God's unfolding purpose through the Jewish people (John 4:22) are preserved to make God's plan known to every thoughtful person who beholds it.

Chapter 18~East of Jordan & Aqaba: Letter No. 13

South of Damascus, the road takes one into a high rolling area known as Bashan in Old Testament times, but now called Hawran. From this point all the way to the river Zered (now called Wady Hasa), flowing from the east-southeast into the south end of the Dead Sea, is a natural grazing land. Its basic character has not changed since Reuben, Gad and half the tribe of Manasseh petitioned Moses that it be given to them for their tribal patrimony because it was an area well-suited to flocks and herds. (See Numbers, chapter 32.) However, today much of the area is cultivated.

The alignment of the main north-south road through Bashan and Gilead remains basically what it has been for millennia. We were assured of that, before reaching Jerash, by Roman mileage markers still standing right beside the present road!

The miles in Gilead were pleasant ones. We sang, "There is a Balm in Gilead" as we savored scenes of fertile rolling hills, dotted with villages, where spring grain had already sprouted, turning countless acres green.

The city of Jerash is the best preserved Roman city in the world. We took a few hours on the way from Ramtha, the Jordanian border crossing where we had spent the night, to Amman to walk through the Temple of Artemis, the Forum, the Theater and to stroll along the stone-paved colonnaded main street of a dead but still beautiful city.

This magnificent amphitheater in Jerash, Jordan, still entirely intact, is a very similar structure to the amphitheater in Ephesus in which a riot against the local Christians was carried out. (See Acts 19:31)

Embarrassingly, for the first time I was able to clearly distinguish between Gerasenes and Gadarenes. The former, referring to the inhabitants of Gerash (or Jerash) and the latter to residents of Gadara, another town of the Decapolis League, which has been almost totally destroyed. Perhaps you can be more indulgent with my ignorance about this distinction when you reflect on the fact, mentioned by Guy P. Duffield in his Handbook of Bible Lands, that the translators of the American Standard Translation of the Bible also were confused by this point. Note the rendering of Mark 5:1: From this it seems one reaches "the country of the Gerasenes" by boat. If the "country" refers to the city and its hinterland, I assure you it is not possible to reach it by sea. Other translations render it, "the country of the Gadarenes" which is harmonious with the location of Gadara.

Several church buildings in Jerash had been built with only a common wall between them, as it were, "tooth by jowl." We wondered if this represented an early form of denominationalism or just concession to the fickle preferences of people. The only doctrinal implication discernible to us from the architectural remains was obvious in the Alpha-Omega medallions carved on several crosses and on one "baptismal" font. What we thought might have been a baptistry is considered by archaeologists to have been only a fountain, probably constructed for

Chapter 18~East of Jordan & Aqaba: Letter No. 13

decorative and aesthetic purposes. One building, adjoining a church and identified by archaeologists as a clubhouse for the choir, gives an interesting insight into the life of the Christians.

The capital of the Ammonites was Rabbath-Ammon (often called Rabbah) which was situated on the site of modern Amman, Jordan. This provides one more of the many arresting examples of the ancient name being preserved till modern times. If one wants tangible evidence of the ancient Ammonite civilization, we think the small Amman Museum is the best place to go. Also in Amman is a great amphitheater from the Roman period which has been restored and is used for concerts in congenial weather.

Our first lodging in Amman (there are no campgrounds) was found finally in the Mansour Hotel after we had trudged up and down, it seemed, innumerable flights of stairs in nine other small cheap-rate hotels. The extreme scarcity of hotel space speaks movingly of the great human tragedy going on in Lebanon.[3] Thousands have fled the carnage, and many of them have sought refuge here. Syria, of course, especially Damascus, is also inundated with many refugees. Prices are high in Jordan, but one consolation is that in Amman and Aqaba, at least, a surprising cornucopia of modern consumer items is available in the shops.

What we call the Anti-Lebanon Mountains (the mountain range on the east side of the Jordan River) is really the uplifted edge of the plateau created by the sinking of the Jordan Valley. That uplifting was augmented by folding and volcanic activity. The great difference in the level of the eastern plateau and the Jordan Valley has given steep gradients to the rivers flowing from the east into the Jordan River and the Dead Sea. All of them have cut magnificent gorges which reach right back to the watershed, which east of the plateau recede gradually into the great Arabian Desert. The watershed is just about where the Hijaz Railway runs, "which skirts the deep wadis to avoid steep gradients and expensive bridges."[4] (The geographical term Hijaz is often spelled Hejaz.) That railway, for any railway buffs among you, was opened in 1908 and was, as you know, romanticized by the daring exploits of Lawrence of Arabia during World War I.

In 1961, a motor road, approximately paralleling the Hijaz Railway as far as Ma'an, was opened from Amman to the Jordanian port of Aqaba. That road is called The Desert Highway, which distinguishes it from "The King's Highway" (Numbers 20:17, 21:22) which is still very much in use. The Hijaz Railway and The Desert Highway are just about on the line which was the eastern border of Moab and Edom.

Many of the steam engines on the Hijaz Railway were manufactured in Switzerland.
~ https://www.flikrcom/photos/thearmaturapress/3505091183, by Mike Bishop 4/28/2009.

From The King's Highway one is rewarded with awesome views of the Arabah. It ties together a host of Biblical sites, the names of which read like an itinerary of Israel's journey to The Land of Milk and Honey. Naturally, we wanted to travel The King's Highway when visibility would be at its best. When we left Amman on January 13th the weather was inclement and visibility poor over the Jordan, so we decided to take the much less historic Desert Highway south to Aqaba and the historic route back, when hopefully visibility would be better. Having completed the circuit last night (I'm continuing this in Amman on January 17th) I report that the visibility remained poor, yet we thank God for what we have seen. For that matter, the poor visibility introduced us to an aspect of the climatology of the area about which we'd read nearly nothing.

While The Desert Highway is not the historic route, it is not devoid of history. There is, of course, the railway. Also, at Jiza (sometimes spelled Ziza) there is an old Roman reservoir holding twenty-three million gallons of water. In recent years it has been repaired and is in regular use. In spite of its tremendous capacity, Glueck says, "One strong rain at the beginning of the rainy season, and the reservoir is full. It supplies the need of … an entire village that has grown up beside it, in addition to the needs of the wayfarers who pass by, or the shepherds who come from considerable distances to water their flocks there."[5] Still, this is the route

Chapter 18~East of Jordan & Aqaba: Letter No. 13

one takes to make a quick journey and to see the desert. We have been in a lot of desert on this trip and have found each area to have a unique beauty.6 As John Bagot Glubb of Middle East fame says so well, "the Arab desert, visualized by many as a horror of desolation, has a loveliness of its own in the vastness of its rolling spaces, the pale blue colour of range after range of faraway hills and the utter silence of its star-lit nights."7

At Ras en Naqab the high desert plateau (ca. 4,000 ft.) ends in a high point called Naqab Ishtar (4,820 ft.) from which one gets a fantastically beautiful view of "rows upon rows of mountains and here and there mountains that resemble icebergs in a vast plain of desert. The plain has pink sand and the hills are red, brown and white."8

From this point the road descends rapidly to the town of Aqaba on the eastern corner of the narrow north end of the Gulf of Aqaba. We had hoped it would be pleasantly warm at this arm of the Red Sea, but were surprised at the strong wind with its high chill factor. The Arabah (which, along with the Jordan Valley and the Orontes Valley in the north and the Gulf of Aqaba to the south, is a part of the great rift which continues into Africa in The Great Rift Valley) acts as a huge wind tunnel. Our few days' experience traveling along the Arabah showed us that a period without wind was merely a time when the wind was changing direction from north to south or vice versa.

The Araba from Rashadiya, Jordan

Heartland of the Middle East

On arrival at Aqaba, Jonathan was feeling a bit nauseated, one of the very few times of off-color health either of us have experienced on this odyssey. So, after a reconnaissance by foot through the small but modern commercial area, we took a room in the Gold Fish Hotel instead of trying to sleep in the Jeep.

Next morning, Jonathan feeling reasonably fit again, we began to take the measure of the place. Here we were in Aqaba! About four miles away, on the opposite corner of the north end of the Gulf, in clear view, gleamed the city of Elat, Israel's Red Sea Port. Between, on the crystal-clear blue water of the Gulf, were riding at anchor more than twenty ships loading or unloading by lighters. In ancient times the Biblical Ezion Geber (Numbers 33:35, I Kings 9:26 et al) was about halfway between the present Aqaba and Elat, but no ruins showed above the sand. (For a fascinating account of the discovery and excavation of Ezion Geber ask your librarian for The Other Side of the Jordan, by Nelson Glueck. His account is in chapter four).

Next, we followed the modern, nearly unused (except during the Haj), four-lane highway twenty kilometers south, right along the edge of the Gulf, to the border of Saudi Arabia. Since there were no good campsites and no shelter from the wind, we gave up the idea of bivouacking in this area to write letters.

Marine life at Jordanian Aqaba is incredibly full of life and color. However, the day we visited, the water was not clear and blocked out color in this photo.

The coral and marine life of the Gulf are unique. The whole world hopes neither Jordan nor Israel will do anything which will destroy the delicate balance of this natural tropical aquarium. We invested six dollars for a private glass-bottomed boat ride in order to photograph a bit of the fantasia of Red Sea marine life.

Shortly after giving our attention to the sea, we again gave it to the desert, retracing our route up the Desert Highway to the first road branching west toward the splendid ruins of Petra, the justly famous Nabataean capital. After a night of rest in the Jeep, we set our priorities. The area covered by all the ruins is extensive. Our time was limited, so we restricted our visit to those tombs one can examine on the way to The High Place where the altars of the ancient city are still intact. From that eyrie one simply marvels at the extent to which the city stretches in the maze of intersecting sandstone canyons. Many, but not all, of the remaining structures are monumental tombs. Just as the expensive burial practices at Palmyra are eloquent

Chapter 18~East of Jordan & Aqaba: Letter No. 13

evidence of the wealth of that city, so the tombs at Petra testify of the riches amassed by the citizens of this ancient emporium.

"Stories of the great wealth of Petra soon caused the Romans to cast covetous eyes in that direction. Two or three attempts to capture the city failed completely, though the Nabataeans as a nation were made to pay tribute. But with all its inaccessibility, it could not hold out against the might of Rome, and in A.D. 106 Petra with all its territory became a Roman Province. The Emperor Trajan built a great road, which passed through Petra, connecting Syria with the Red Sea. Under Roman rule Petra prospered greatly, and some of the finest monuments date from this period. ... More and more wealth was lavished on the city, foreign craftsmen were brought in to embellish and beautify it, and it became one of the wonders of the world."9

There is order, hope and promise at the end of the defile.

There is hardly any place in Jordan that is not connected with biblical history, and Petra is no exception. Paul's narrow escape from the Jews in Damascus was especially precarious because the Jews had apparently persuaded the governor (*ethnarch*) appointed by King Aretas to also throw the police into the manhunt. (See Acts 9:23, II Corinthians 11:32-33.) The King was the Nabataean Aretas IV, whose capital was Petra. It was the daughter of this same king whom Herod Antipas had divorced to marry Herodias, his brother Philip's wife.

The wealth of the city of Petra came, in part, from export of indigenous products. Those were "gold, silver, copper, and sesame oil. They [also] exported the asphalt from the Dead Sea (it was used in Egypt for embalming) while they worked the copper mines in the Wadi Araba."10 The greater part of their wealth, however, came from tolls levied on incense and spice caravans for safe passage rights through their territory. "From the end of the fourth century (B.C.) on, Petra became a key city on the caravan route, linking spice-producing South Arabia with the consuming and marketing centres in the north. It commanded the routes to the port of Gaza in the west, to Busra and Damascus in the north, to Aila (the Nabataean port on the north shore of the Gulf of Aqaba about three kilometers east of ancient Ezion Geber) on the Red Sea, and to the Persian Gulf across the desert. In it the relays of camels were provided."[11] A third source of wealth in Roman times came from a Roman subsidy to Nabatea for its role as an allied buffer state.

The security which the rocky crags of Petra offered made it an inviting city site. The main entrance, called the sig, is a perpendicular walled natural serpentine cleft in the sandstone, which narrows to eight feet and is some 300 feet deep. It could be held by a handful of brave men. Hitti mentions another very strong reason for establishing a city in such a difficult place. "Theirs was the only town between the Jordan and Al-Hijaz which had not only abundant but invitingly pure water."[12] When need arose they supplemented that natural supply by some of the most amazing hydraulic engineering of all time. As Hitti further suggests, they seem almost to have inherited Moses' rod! The defensibility of the site generated pride in the Edomites, predecessors of the Nabataeans and successors to the Horites.[13]

During the reign of the Emperor Trajan, probably in Rome's preparation to test the strength of the Parthian Empire to the east, the Kingdom of Petra was swallowed up and made part of the Roman province of Arabia. (This is most probably the Arabia to which Paul traveled; see Galatians 1:17.)

Under the Romans, "the east-to-west trade route shifted north to Palmyra, the south-to-north moved east to where the Moslem pilgrimage road and the modern Hijaz Railway lie."[14] Petra's glory was past. Centuries later, it was the scene of battles between Muslims and Crusaders. Then, "the very memory of Petra was lost, its situation forgotten, it was a legend. Explorers tried

The Treasury at Petra.

Chapter 18~East of Jordan & Aqaba: Letter No. 13

to find it, but it kept its secret for years. Finally in August 1812 Johann Ludwig Burckhardt stood within it. He was the first European in centuries to look upon the fallen wonder that was Petra and return to tell the world."[15] One hundred sixty-four years after Burckhardt, as swarms of other tourists have, Jonathan and I stood within it and thanked God for deepened insight into the working out of His eternal purpose.

Climbing the steep road out of Petra, we regained The King's Highway on the rim of the Arabah. The highway traverses many wadis (gulches) flowing into the Arabah, so inevitably one encounters steep gradients as the road twists down, into, and up out of the wadis. Our goal was two-fold, to see as much of the Arabah as possible and to reach Bozra, the capital of ancient Edom. To get a spectacular view of the Arabah, we were rushing along to get to an ideal spot just before descending to the police post at Rashadiya. Unfortunately, we missed a turn a short way out of Shaubak and made it almost back to The Desert Highway before we realized we were going the wrong way! We found it an instructive experience anyway. Most of the farming in ancient Edom, as today, took place in a narrow belt paralleling the brink of the Arabah. A bit east of it, the land levels out into high plains, but only that higher, narrowly twisting ribbon gets enough rainfall to support regular agriculture.

Retracing our way toward Shaubak we pressed on toward Rashadiya, only a short while before sunset. The magnificence of the vast Arabah rift was enhanced by the magical evening light. We went by foot—through thistles that make California star thistles seem benign—to the brink for pictures, then back to the Jeep against a strong wind pouring over the edge and down the rift.

On to Bozra. The name of Bozra is preserved in the name of the village of Buseira, near the ancient site. We had been rather successful so far in bird-dogging old ruins, but the Edomites proved elusive. Off the main road, into Buseira, to the end of the road and back again. No Bozra. Now the wind was almost a gale. We determined to camp in the Jeep in a wide spot just off the road and search for Bozra in the morning.

While heating a can of soup (which came from a fabulous store in Amman), a car —lights ablaze—pulled in at right angles to our Jeep. It was the Inspector of Police for the area, Captain Yasin. He'd seen us slowly driving in and out of Buseira and now camped along the road. He emphasized that the area was unsettled and unsafe. He requested us not to stay the night by the road but to come into Tafila after our meal (the ancient Tophel, Deuteronomy 1:1) where he assured us there was a hotel.

On arrival, there were no lights in the town due to a complete failure of the municipal generating station. The only establishment with a sign was a tea shop.

Heartland of the Middle East

We could find neither a hotel nor the police post. Back up the hill to the tea shop. Just before reaching it, a rear rim split on the Jeep for the 10th or 12th time (we've lost count) and, being pushed out by the pressure in the tire, began thumping on the frame at each revolution. The young proprietor, Ahmad Owamer, was a model of Arab hospitality. "Yes, there is a hotel. I'll call the man in charge. In the meantime you must have tea." It was excellent. After about an hour's wait the young man in charge of the municipal hotel arrived and we, the only guests, were shown to our room. Two or three young fellows, friends of the manager, stayed in an adjoining room, apparently just so we'd not be alone in the building.

Next morning we were not permitted to pay for the good breakfast of omelettes and tea. Ahmad, our host, then showed us the tire shop and the welding shop where we began what had now become a ritual, dismounting the tires, straightening and welding the rims, and remounting the tires. Back to the search for Bozra. Slowly all the way to Buseira again. Back to the main road again. No luck. We read our guide book again. We'd done everything right, but no Bozra.

Stopping to let Jonathan check the trailer tires, I looked casually out of the driver's side window. Suddenly, I realized that what had appeared to be only a haphazard jumble of stone really was the remnant of old walls. After assuming failure, quite casually it seemed, we found the object of our quest. Such destruction, that even expressive photography is difficult! God said the palaces of Bozra would be devoured (Amos 1:12). He said it would "become an astonishment, a reproach, a waste and a curse" (Jeremiah 49:13). This is what remains of the proud capital that refused visas to Moses and his people (Numbers 20:14-21).

Later, while here at Karak, I read all the biblical passages about Bozra. "The line of confusion and the plummet of emptiness" (Isaiah 34:11) have surely been stretched over it. Both of us were awe-stricken with the unmistakable accuracy. So much so, that we passed three times without recognizing that its ruins were there! "No man shall dwell there" (Jeremiah 49:18). We couldn't stay even one night! The police fear the place. "It shall be ... a court for ostriches" (Isaiah 34:13). Ostriches! Somehow I'd never really thought of ostriches as part of the biblical fauna. Then suddenly, two things from the collections in the Amman Museum took on new and startling relevance for me. First, a large ostrich egg found among the burial objects from a Jericho tomb, and secondly an early Semitic inscribed picture of an ostrich from a short way north of Amman. The biblical prophecy, in light of those two artifacts, didn't seem so impossible of fulfillment after all. I was surprised I had previously read nothing pertinent about ostriches in Palestine. And I was surprised by my surprise at the prophecy! I thought, "Just what was the situation in Palestine and Edom regarding that queer bird?" Hoade, in discussing the fauna of the area, gave the statistic I was search-

Chapter 18~East of Jordan & Aqaba: Letter No. 13

ing for: "The ostrich to be met with Jubal Tubaig (ca. 100 miles east-southeast of Bozra) until about 1932, has retreated into Saudi Arabia."[16]

> From your companions,
> on the True King's Highway (Is 35:8)
> With Love,
> Lee and Jonathan

P.S. (Added November 30, 2020): Since the Hijaz Railway became extremely important in the World War I allied tactical decisions, an additional brief note is certainly justified. Turkey allied itself with Germany in World War I on October 29, 1914. Because of Turkey's Hijaz Railway, it theoretically made it possible for Germany to transport heavy, long-range artillery to Turkey's town of Aqaba at the north end of the Gulf of Aqaba. That would have made it impossible for Great Britain to continue use of the Suez Canal which had been opened for international use on November 17, 1869.

Only a few years before the beginning of World War I, Great Britain converted its entire world-wide navy from a coal-burning to an oil-burning fleet. The supply of oil for Britain's Mediterranean and Atlantic naval fleets came from oil fields in Iran. Had Germany succeeded in putting long-range artillery in place at Aqaba she could have sunk each and every British oil tanker, thus ending the British navy's tremendous contribution to Allied victory in World War I.

Turkey's Hijaz Railway ran from Damascus, Syria, to Medina in Saudi Arabia, a distance of 820 miles.[17] It was not only a great boon to Muslim devotees on their pilgrimage to Medina and Mecca, but stimulated economic activity on both sides of the railway for the entire distance covered by its tracks. Many of the railway engines were powered by burning wood in their fireboxes. The massive cutting of wood for fuel had begun to stimulate ecological criticism. "The British spy T. E. Lawrence, who met Faisal in October 1916, masterminded the sabotage of the Hijaz Railway."[18]

"Without having gained Akaba, [the town of Akaba/Aqaba on the north end of the Red Sea Gulf of Akaba] which was the last base in safe water; and in my judgment the only door, except the Middle Euphrates, which we could unlock for an assuredly successful entry into Syria.

"Akaba's special value to the Turks was that, when they pleased, it might be constituted a threat to the right flank of the British Army. At the end of 1914 their higher command had thought to make it their main route to the [Suez] Canal: but they found the food and water difficulties great, and adopted the Beersheba route. Now, however, the British had left the Canal positions and had thrust forward to Gaza and Beersheba. This made the feeding of the Turkish army easier by shortening its line. Consequently, the Turks had surplus transport. Akaba was also of greater geographical value than of old, since it now lay behind the British right, and a small force operating from it would threaten either El Arish or Suez effectively. ... We organized the Akaba area as an unassailable base, from which to hinder the Hijaz Railway."[19]

---

1   "The term 'Jordan Valley' often applies just to the lower course of the Jordan River, from the spot where it exits the Sea of Galilee in the north, to the end of its course where it flows into the Dead Sea in the south. In a wider sense, the term may also cover the Dead Sea basin and the Arabah valley, which is the rift valley segment beyond the Dead Sea and ending at Aqaba/Eilat, 155 km (96 mi) farther south." ~ https://en.wikipedia.org/wiki/Jordan_Valley (Accessed 5/7/21.)
2   Consequently, hotel rooms, particularly in Amman, were in very short supply.
3   Fighting in Beirut between "Christian" Phalangists and Muslims had, since October 1st 1975, become very intense and had spread to many areas outside Beirut. On January 8th and 14th a total of three Palestinian refugee camps were captured by the Phalangists. Many who were able to do so had fled from Lebanon to Damascus and to Amman for safety.
4   Eugene Hoade, East of the Jordan, (Jerusalem: Franciscan Printing Press, 1966), p. 19.
5   Nelson Glueck, The Other Side of the Jordan, (New Haven: American Schools of Oriental Research, 1940), p. 35.
6   A later note on this point seems justified. Beauty, to some extent, must be in the eye of the beholder—though I contend it lies to some degree also in the object. But one may make himself oblivious to beauty, especially if it should be accompanied by discomforting liabilities such as heat, dust, or insects. One who expressed a view contrary to the one I hold, and that expressed by John Bagot Glubb, is the American spy and espionage expert, Kermit Roosevelt. He wrote of the Syrian desert between Damascus and the Iraq border. "We...left in the comparative cool of the evening to take the pipeline road for Baghdad. You miss nothing driving that road at night—except heat and glare and long miles of rock and sand." Kermit Roosevelt, Counter Coup, The Struggle for the Control of Iran, (New York McGraw-Hill Book Company, 1979), p. 138-139.
7   John Bagot Glubb, The Way of Love, (London: Hodder and Stoughton, 1974), p. 45.
8   Eugene Hoade, East of the Jordan, (Jerusalem: Franciscan Printing Press, 1966), p. 224.
9   Author not given, Petra, A Brief History & Some Photographs, (Amman, Jordan: Jordan Distribution Agency, 1973), pp. 31-32.
10 Eugene Hoade, East of the Jordan, (Jerusalem: Franciscan Printing Press, 1966), p. 221.
11 Philip K. Hitti, History of Syria, (London: Macmillan & Co. Ltd., 1957), p. 377.
    A later reading note cites an important additional dimension of the trade through this once great entrepot: "When we come to the first evidence from Chinese sources of commerce with the West ... in 128 and 91 B.C., it is clear that much, if not all of the Chinese silk was sent by sea from the Persian Gulf to the Nabataean Arabs at their ports on the Red Sea, and so to Petra and through to Palestine and Syria." – George Every, Understanding Eastern Christianity, (London: SCM Press Ltd., 1978), p. 21.
12 Philip K. Hitti, History of Syria, (London: Macmillan & Co. Ltd., 1957), p. 376.
13 See Jeremiah 49:16, "the rock" - Hebrew, 'Sela' is Petra, the rock. One of the chief gods of the Nabataeans was Dhu-esh-Shera, "meaning He-of-Shera. The Shera are the mountains of the Petra region, the Seir of Genesis 14:6." – Philip K. Hitti, History of Syria, (London: Macmillan & Co. Ltd., 1957), p. 220.
14 Philip K. Hitti, History of Syria, (London: Macmillan & Co. Ltd., 1957), p. 382.
15 Eugene Hoade, East of the Jordan, (Jerusalem: Franciscan Printing Press, 1966), p. 219.
16 Eugene Hoade, East of the Jordan, (Jerusalem: Franciscan Printing Press, 1966), p. 31.
    The famous T.E. Lawrence tells us in his classic book, Seven Pillars of Wisdom, "At dawn there came in five men of the Sherarat from the desert east of Tebuk, bringing a present of eggs of the Arabian ostrich, plentiful in their little frequented desert. ... As we went, some little puffs of dust scurried into the eye of wind. Auda said they were ostriches. A man ran up to us with two great ivory eggs. We settled to breakfast on this bounty of the Biscipa, and looked for fuel, but in twenty minutes found only a wisp of grass. The barren desert was defeating us. The baggage train passed and my eye fell on the loads of blasting gelatine. We broached a packet, shedding it carefully into a fire beneath the egg propped on stones, till the

Chapter 18~East of Jordan & Aqaba: Letter No. 13

cookery was pronounced complete. Nasir and Nesib, really interested, dismounted to scoff at us. Auda drew his silver-hilted dagger and chipped the top of the first egg. A stink like a pestilence went across our party. We fled to a clean spot, rolling the second egg hot before us with gentle kicks. It was fresh enough, and hard as a stone. We dug out its contents with the dagger onto the flint flakes which were our platters, and ate it piece-meal, persuading even Nasir, who in his life before had never fallen so low as egg-meat, to take his share. The general verdict was: tough and strong, but good in the Biscipa." – T.E. Lawrence, Seven Pillars of Wisdom, a Triumph, (Jonathan Cape, Privately printed, 1926), p. 180 & 259.

17 Elizabeth F. Thompson, How the West Stole Democracy from the Arabs, (Atlantic Monthly Press, New York, 2020), p. 3.
18 Elizabeth F. Thompson, How the West Stole Democracy from the Arabs, (Atlantic Monthly Press, New York, 2020), p. 6.
19 T.E. Lawrence, Seven Pillars of Wisdom, a Triumph, (Jonathan Cape, Privately printed, 1926), p. 281-321.

Chapter 19

John & Moses Called Home

Homeward-Bound Letter No. 14
Aleppo, Syria
February 4, 1976

Dear Friends,

The hotel manager at Karak assured us we could get permission within fifteen minutes from the governor to visit El Lisan. His office was just a few doors away. However, since the military presence the previous evening had been so obvious and the control so tight, we judged a stay on The Tongue jutting into the Dead Sea could only be brief and that under such close scrutiny that spontaneity and carefreeness would be largely ruled out. Learning that one could drive without restriction to the north end of the Dead Sea by a route through Madaba and Na'ur and then via the Amman-Jerusalem road, we opted for that alternative.

Still following The King's Highway, the millenia-old route through [biblical] Moab, we set our course for Madaba. We also projected a side trip to Machaerus, Herod Antipas' gruesome keep, overlooking the Dead Sea, the place of John the Baptist's imprisonment and execution. Between Karak and the Machaerus turn-off, one passes through Heshbon and Diban, the latter is one site where the Moabites' stone was recovered.[1] As fascinating as the ruins are, one must set priorities when time is limited. So, with stops only for general photos of the sites, we pressed on.

The turn-off for Machaerus is well marked, but after driving some twenty-two kilometers to the village of Mukkawir the road simply ended. Friendly villagers indicated that a dirt track a couple of kilometers back was the right way. It ended in a diametrically wrong direction, at a peasant's hut. Fortunately we'd noticed another dirt and rock track between the two routes we'd explored. Since it was the only alternative, off we went. A fork in the road complicated matters momentarily, but consensus was in favor of the left branch. It descended steeply in the direction of the Dead Sea, which was encouraging. A Bedouin assured us that we were on the right way to Meshraus, the local name for Machaerus, and that we should park at the spot nearest his tent.

The conical mountain with ruins of Machaerus

Heartland of the Middle East

Shortly, the conical mountain with ruins of Machaerus loomed close and to the right of the black goat-haired tent of our Bedouin friend. The rough road went on very steeply toward its rendezvous with the Salten Sea. We assessed it as a military road that could be put in shape with some gravel and a few passes of a road grader. There was no wide spot nor turn-around where we needed to stop, so the trailer had to be unhitched for the maneuver. Almost as if by magic, three local lads, obviously brothers, presented themselves and offered to show us the trail to the ruins. They asked no remuneration and probably expected none. It has been our delight to reward just such spontaneously helpful, unselfish non-professionals.

As we finished clambering over the ruins of Machaerus, evening shadows were already deepening down near our Jeep. We would, we decided, make the short drive into Madaba where, after spending the night, we'd see the famous Madaba map and then visit Nebo before descending via Na'ur to the Asphalt Sea. We knew there was a government rest house in the town. We were surprised to find there was no other hotel and the rest house offered no sleeping facilities. Had we known the situation at Nebo, we would have driven there to spend the night in our Jeep. We were told that towns close enough for one to drive to Amman did not have hotels. So we made our way some thirty miles back to Amman and to the Mansour Hotel again.

We had planned to get permission for re-entry into Syria at the border crossing. Since the tension because of the Lebanon tragedy had increased very perceptibly in the past few days, we judged it would be prudent to get a visa from the Syrian embassy rather than rely on chancy border permission. Also, since our experience with a military road block on the El Lisan Road, we thought it advisable to get information about the section of the Jordan Valley Road between the Dead Sea and Irbid. The Royal Automobile Association in Amman assured us there would be no problem.

After two and a half days in Amman, our business finished, we made our way again to Madaba. About halfway there, for the umpteenth time, a rear rim split and bulged out, hitting the frame at each revolution. Putting on our last spare, we made our way to Madaba with changed priorities. They had been to visit the Madaba map and make a straight course to Nebo, a very short drive from Madaba. Now, it was to find a tire shop and a welding shop. The welding was getting three or four layers deep. Obviously, something else would have to be done before long.

On our way to Nebo,
Lee and Jonathan

---

1   The Moabite Stone gives the Moabite King Mesha's account of relations with Israel from the reign of Israel's King Omri to the reign of King Jehoram, against whom Mesha rebelled (cf. II Kings 3:4-27). The statement in II Kings 3:27, "And there was great wrath against Israel: and they departed from him, and returned to their own land," seems to confirm, at least to some extent, the claim to victory which King Mesha made in the inscription on the Moabite Stone.

Chapter 20

A Cosmopolitan City for a Cosmopolitan Gospel

Homeward-Bound Letter No. 15
Antakya, Turkey
February 8, 1976

Dear Friends,

Tonight we are lodging on the Orontes River in the Kent Hotel [in Antakya], one of the few cities in Turkey whose name has not undergone such a metamorphosis that it no longer bears any resemblance to its classical or biblical name. We are in Antakya, the Antioch of Acts chapter thirteen, the home of what will very probably prove to have been the most evangelistic church in the whole history of Christianity.

Army General Seleucus Nicator (the Victor), later known as Seleucus I, had succeeded, after the death of Alexander the Great, in grasping the choicest parts of that great conqueror's conquests. He founded Antioch in 312 B.C., or thereabouts, and named it in honor of his father Antiochus. Seleucus felt his new empire (the Seleucid) should have a new capital. Rejecting venerable capitals within his empire: Ecbatana, Babylon, and Sardis, to mention only three, he founded, here on the Orontes River, a splendid capital city. However, Seleucia, a very close derivative of Seleucus, the older capital on the Tigris, was not abandoned and continued to function.

From their new center, the Seleucid kings spread Hellenism with evangelical zeal. In spite of their efforts, Hellenism remained only a veneer in most of the empire. However, it did establish the Greek language as a *lingua franca* which became a very important means of making the Gospel known to the whole "civilized" world.

In marked contrast to the superficial impact of Greek culture propagated from Antioch, the influence of the Gospel of Christ radiating from this same center was infinitely more profound. As Hellenism made its unsuccessful bid for world conquest from this then-sumptuous city, the Gospel of Christ, through the vision and dedication of the congregation here, began its triumphant worldwide conquest "unto the uttermost part of the earth" (Acts 1:8). Thus, Antioch became the center for the very important fourth stage of that conquest which Jesus predicted, as recorded in Acts 1:8. Since the ministry of Christ's Gospel was to be worldwide, it was appropriate that its great mission to the Gentile world should begin from such a cosmopolitan city as Antioch was at that time.

Because our itinerary had become very crowded due to time lost in working on the Jeep, we had no opportunity to explore the city of Antioch thoroughly, therefore I share fine descriptions from others who wrote later. Antioch, on the Orontes River was "a scenic, well-provisioned river city at the foot of a majestic mountain, with a colonnaded downtown grid and an ample supply of stadiums and gardens, monumental fountains and natural springs. Bathed in westerly breezes from May to October, Antioch was sunny and windless in winter, with delightful baths and a lively market."[1] "In Antioch, then the largest city in the near east, he [Herod] paved the main street, 2.5 miles long, providing colonnades the whole length to shelter its citizens from the rain, and finished this great work in polished marble."[2] To the south, Antioch also had an associated nearby cantonment, Apamea, named for Seleucus Nicator's beautiful Persian wife.

Not only was there propriety in the wider mission of Christ's Gospel beginning from Antioch, but irony as well. As all of you know from reading Lew Wallace's Ben Hur, Antioch and nearby Daphne were centers of sensuality. Hitti puts the situation straight with an economy of words, "The palm for luxurious and dissolute living goes to Antioch with its suburb Daphne. Nowhere else in Roman Syria does the enjoyment of life seem to have been the goal and the duties of life the side issue as in this North Syrian spot."[3] Yet, ironically, it was from this place, given to sensual pleasure, that the Gospel of Christ which reasons "of righteousness, and self-control, and the judgment to come" (Acts 24:25) went forth conquering and to conquer.

Irrigation water is so needed that aqueducts carry it through the city of Hama.

While on the subject of the Orontes River, it seems appropriate to mention that our first contact with it was at Hama (Hamath of Scripture, II Chronicles 8:3-4) on our way north from Jordan to Turkey. At Hama we made a point to visit some of its world-famous water wheels of enormous diameter which lift the Orontes

Chapter 20~A Cosmopolitan City for a Cosmopolitan Gospel: Letter No. 15

River water into high aqueducts which carry it on its life-giving mission to many orchards and gardens.

One of Hama's famous waterwheels in a rural area.

Of all Syrian cities we've seen, we think Hama has the most individuality and character. But, like all the cities of Syria, it does need far more adequate garbage collection and disposal services. In the small Hama Museum we found a beautiful early fourth-century mosaic floor depicting a group of performing musicians. We were amazed to see exquisitely portrayed musical bowls and a portable pipe organ, as well as the harp and other instruments more usually associated with the period.

From Hama we drove back to Aleppo to work on the Jeep. We had noticed it was the most auto-oriented city encountered on our trip. We felt if parts and services could be had anywhere, Aleppo was the spot. Aleppo could probably take the prize for being the most drab city in Syria, although it does have a splendid museum, and a very impressive citadel, which we've mentioned before. Also, its old covered bazaar is the most genuinely oriental bazaar we have visited. It is not slanted toward tourists, but is a truly living mercantile institution of very large size, offering an amazing variety of merchandise. Otherwise, Aleppo is dreary and drab and the underground storage garage where we rented space to work on the

Jeep must be one of the dreariest places in that drab city. After eight days' dedicated effort, Jonathan and I were happy to bid farewell to Aleppo and be on the road again.

Our route took us south to the magnificent ruins of Apamea, the second most glorious city of the Seleucid Empire. It was the western imperial cantonment city of the Seleucids. It too, was founded by Seleucus I, but, as mentioned before, named in honor of his Persian wife Apame. He had married her in Alexander's mass marriage of his officers to Persian women in his quest for "homoneia," as Alexander termed his effort to blend the Greek and Persian people. It is noteworthy that Seleucus is the only one who did not divorce his wife following Alexander's death.

The beautiful swirled columns at Apamea

Apamea is situated on the Syrian plateau just before it breaks abruptly away toward the right or east bank of the Orontes. It was a magnificent Hellenistic city, built typically on the grid system, the main streets flanked by colonnades.

The colonnades are unique because the pillars have swirled fluting. We have often marveled, while beholding columns from Persepolis to the Mediterranean, how the builders could make the fluting so accurate and uniform without distortion from one pillar drum to the next. But to make the fluting spiral up the columns, as it does at Apamea, must evoke the admiration of the most grudging beholder! In any case, we couldn't spend much time at Apamea. Because the weather was inclement we cut our visit short, indeed. Even so, the sun obliged us by lighting some of the columns for a quick photo or two. Then, after choosing a few Greek and Roman coins from a selection offered by local shepherd girls, we hurried on to reach Latakia for the night

Just a few hundred yards to the west of Apamea, the road drops steeply down the rocky upraised edge of the Syrian plateau into the flat but beautiful Orontes River Valley. The valley's lush green carpet was balm to our eyes after the muddy gray monotony of Aleppo. The valley floor, stretching some three to five miles to the base of the Lebanon Mountains in the west, was so flat it tended to be marshy at times. We also wondered if malaria might not be a problem here because of poor

Chapter 20~A Cosmopolitan City for a Cosmopolitan Gospel: Letter No. 15

drainage. Still, intensive farming of the rich black alluvium was obviously carried on, though spring here had not advanced far enough for us to recognize which crops were being grown.

Hurrying north in the rainy dusk, we paralleled the Orontes River till we intersected the road from Aleppo to Latakia. Then, turning southwest, we climbed the steep twisting pass over the Lebanon Range as fingers of lightning traced their erratic paths in the sky just to the north.

As we descended from the Lebanon Range to the coast, the climate continued to moderate. It was bracing but mild in Latakia, Syria's largest seaport (sometimes maps identify Latakia by its Arabic name: Al Ladhiqiyah). Sixteen years earlier, on our first trip to Pakistan, our ship had docked here for some twenty-four hours. On that occasion I had preached, with the help of a translator, at the Reformed Presbyterian Church building to a small Turkish Christian group which met in that facility. Sixteen years had brought change. The morning after our arrival was Sunday and we strolled along the waterfront where the Mediterranean was running high before a stiff breeze. It was unfortunate, to say the least, that because of time lost on repairing the Jeep we were not able once again to worship with those Turkish Christians.

After a light lunch we made for the ruins of the ancient Canaanite city of Ugarit, some six or seven miles north of Latakia. Rain made photography difficult and forced us to make our tour of the ruins brief. Still, we became reacquainted with the impressive remnants of that important Canaanite city which we had visited sixteen years earlier.

Archaeologist Philip K. Hitti helps all of us understand the significance of the discovery of the ruins of the ancient Canaanite city of Ugarit. In a very terse and brief resumé, he wrote: "Among texts found since the 1930s, besides the collections of cuneiform tablets from the Mesopotamian Bronze Age city of Mari on the upper Euphrates, are those from the Bronze Age city of Ugarit in northern Syria and now also Ebla of special interest to us, in view of the significant and wide comparative background they provide on social, religious, literary and other aspects."[4]

Latakia is Syria's largest seaport. Only 85 kilometers to the south of Latakia is Tartus, a small deep-water port, home to Russia's Mediterranean naval fleet, its only naval base on the Mediterranean. Also, not far from Latakia is a military air base whose name is Khmeimim, now being used by Russia.

While I conclude the description of the Middle Eastern part of our journey with this letter, Jonathan and I had to rush on through Europe, with stops at several great World War I battlefields in France. We traveled on to London to visit with our shortwave broadcast station operators, then put our old Jeep on a boat. We then flew to Boston, traveled to New York to pick the Jeep up, and began our trip across America for a delightful reunion with my wife, Gerry, and our youngest daughter, Joanna, in Portland, Oregon.

> With love,
> Lee and Jonathan

P.S. As soon as Jonathan and I crossed from Turkey to Greece, we realized we were unmistakably in a new and different environment. On the Greek roads, every few miles, are little roadside chapels, like this one, inviting the traveler to break his journey long enough to pray to God through Christ!

---

1. Stacy Schiff, <u>Cleopatra, A Life</u>, (New York: Little, Brown & Co., 2010), p. 191. The same author said, "Antioch was 'a miniature, less profligate version of Alexandria.'" <u>op.cit</u>. p. 190.
2. Paul Johnson, <u>A History of the Jews</u>, (NY: Harper Perennial, 1987), p. 113.
3. Philip K. Hitti, <u>History of Syria</u>, (London: Macmillan & Co. Ltd., 1957), p. 268.
4. B.S.J. Isserlin, <u>The Israelites</u>, (London: Thames and Hudson, 1998), p. 13.

Epilogue

The tragedy of civil war in Syria has drawn Russia in a major way into the area. They have refurbished their largely unused naval base, making it a living military factor in the eastern Mediterranean. As all of you know, it is due to the activities of Russia's forces in Syria that Bashar al-Assad (the rapacious Syrian dictator) has been able to stay in power. Syria has been horribly damaged because of the war. Iran, in its insatiable desire to push to the Mediterranean, has also supported Bashar al-Assad. Though the fighting between Assad's forces and the rebels is largely finished, and the rebels have either been killed, imprisoned or driven out, Iran is still trying to dominate the area. Iran's attempt to bring in supplies to build military bases has been largely thwarted by the Israeli Air Force.

We all need to pray about where the ongoing struggle in Syria will ultimately lead. A new dimension is seen by Russia using its naval base to support its involvement in the Libyan Civil War in North Africa. As of June 7, 2020 the forces in Libya's current civil war led by Khalifa Hifter, with the support of Russia, has suffered a major military defeat by forces supported by Turkey. Undoubtedly, these desperate, ruthless events will in due time lead to a much wider war in the Middle East. I have put that war in the context of biblical prophecy in a book entitled <u>The Definitive Battle for Palestine</u>.

Heartland of the Middle East

Atlas

Map of the Area Traveled

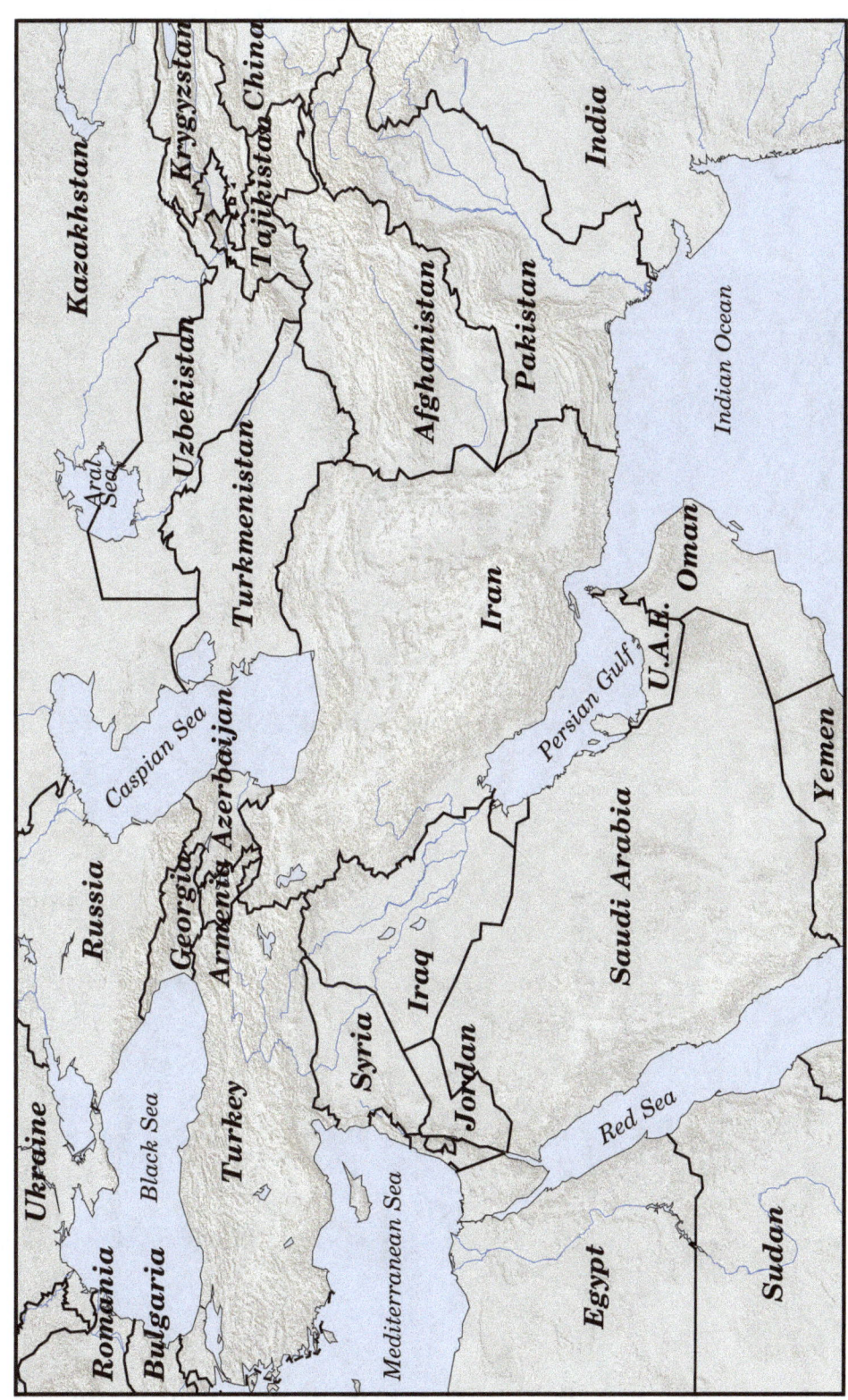

Heartland of the Middle East

Map of Pakistan

Atlas

Map of Afghanistan

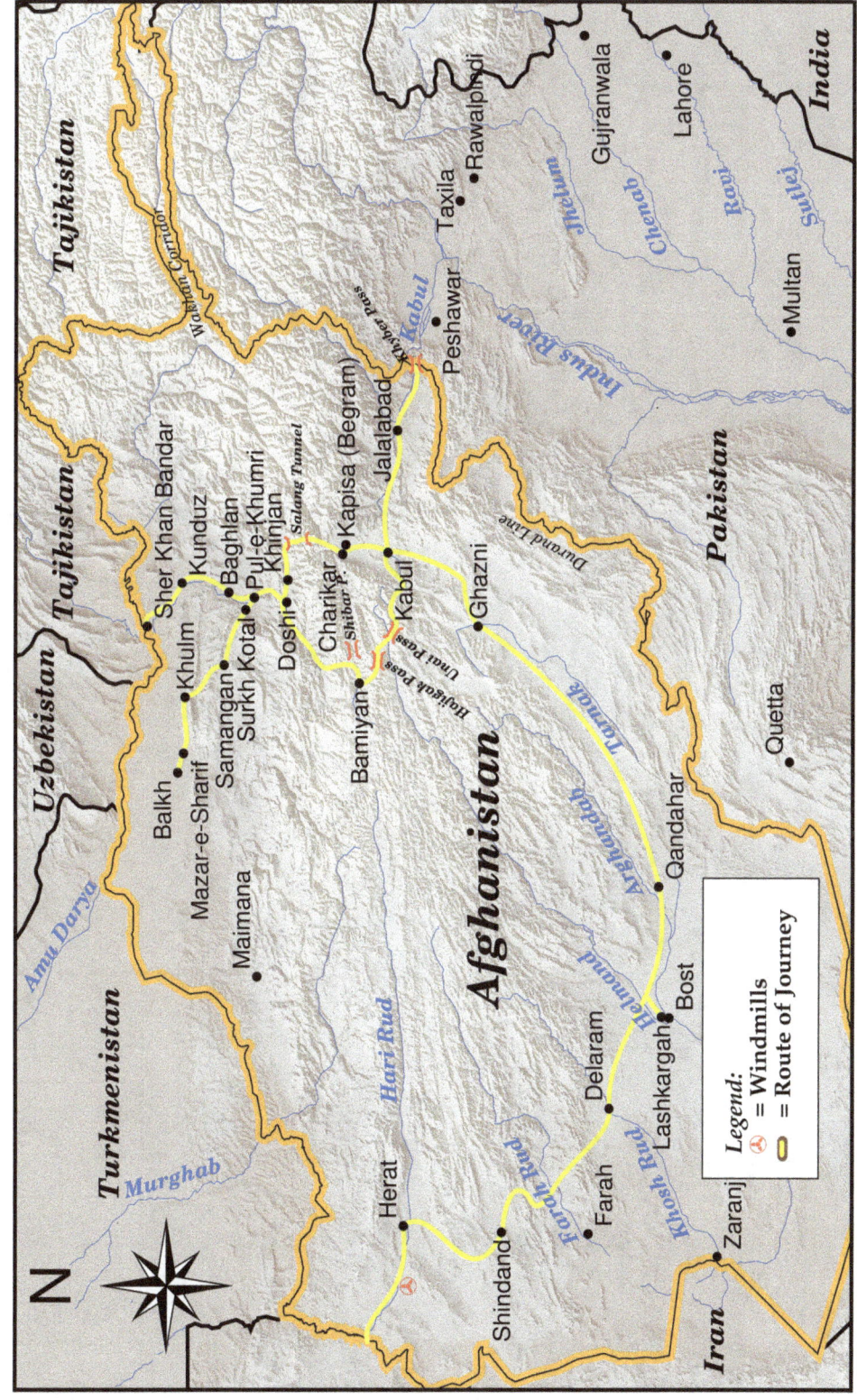

Heartland of the Middle East

Map of Iran

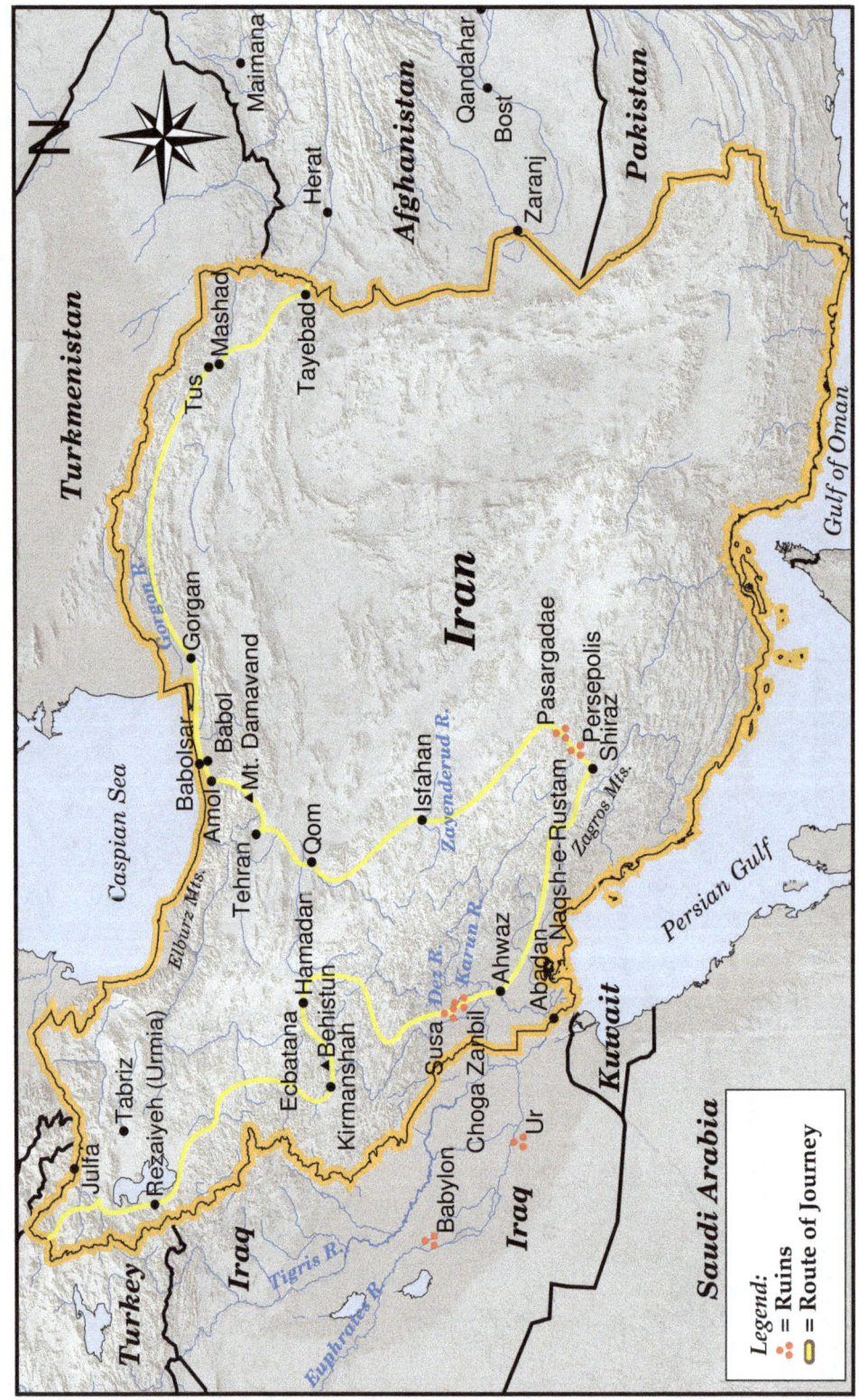

Atlas

Map of Syria

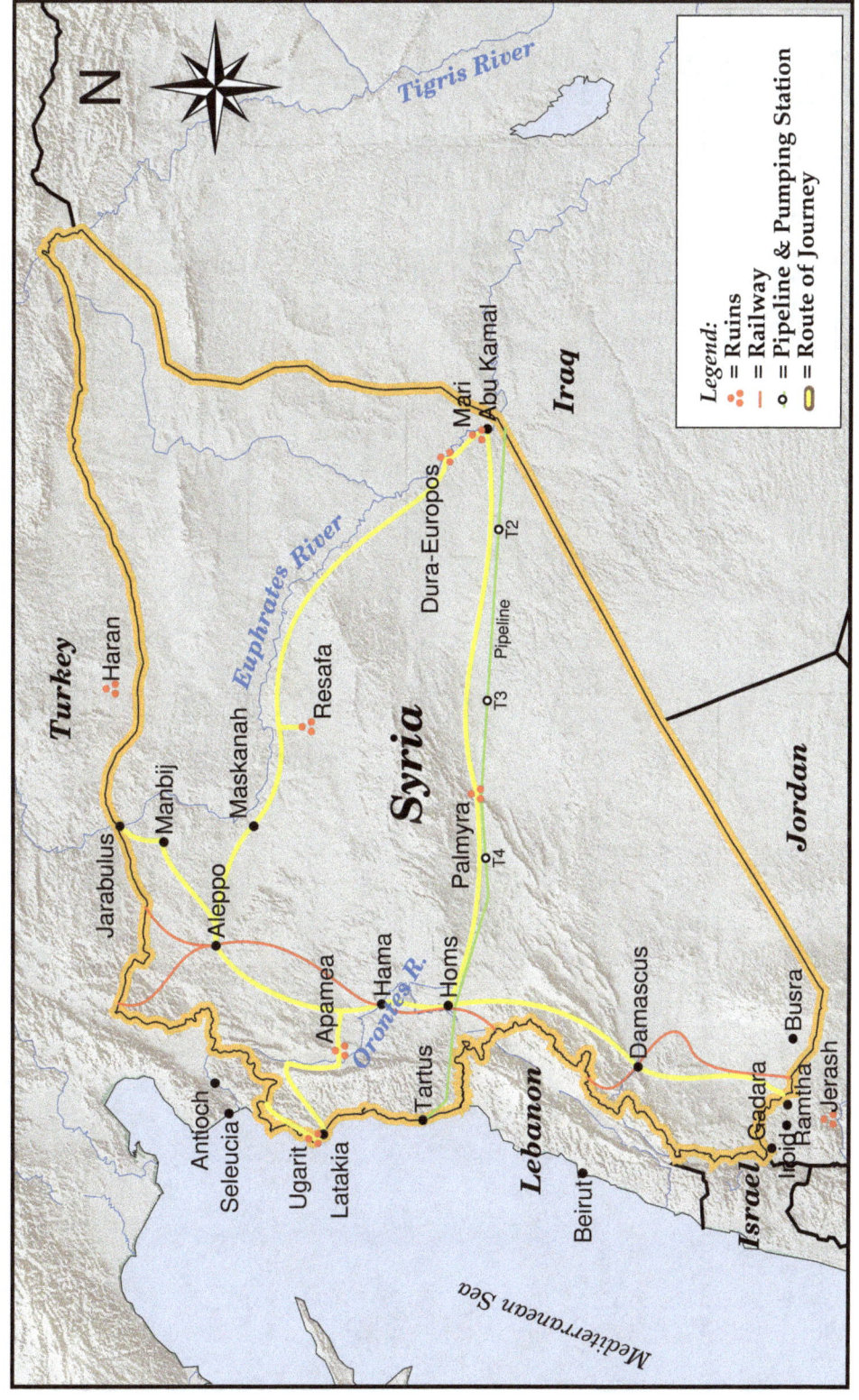

Heartland of the Middle East

Map of Turkey

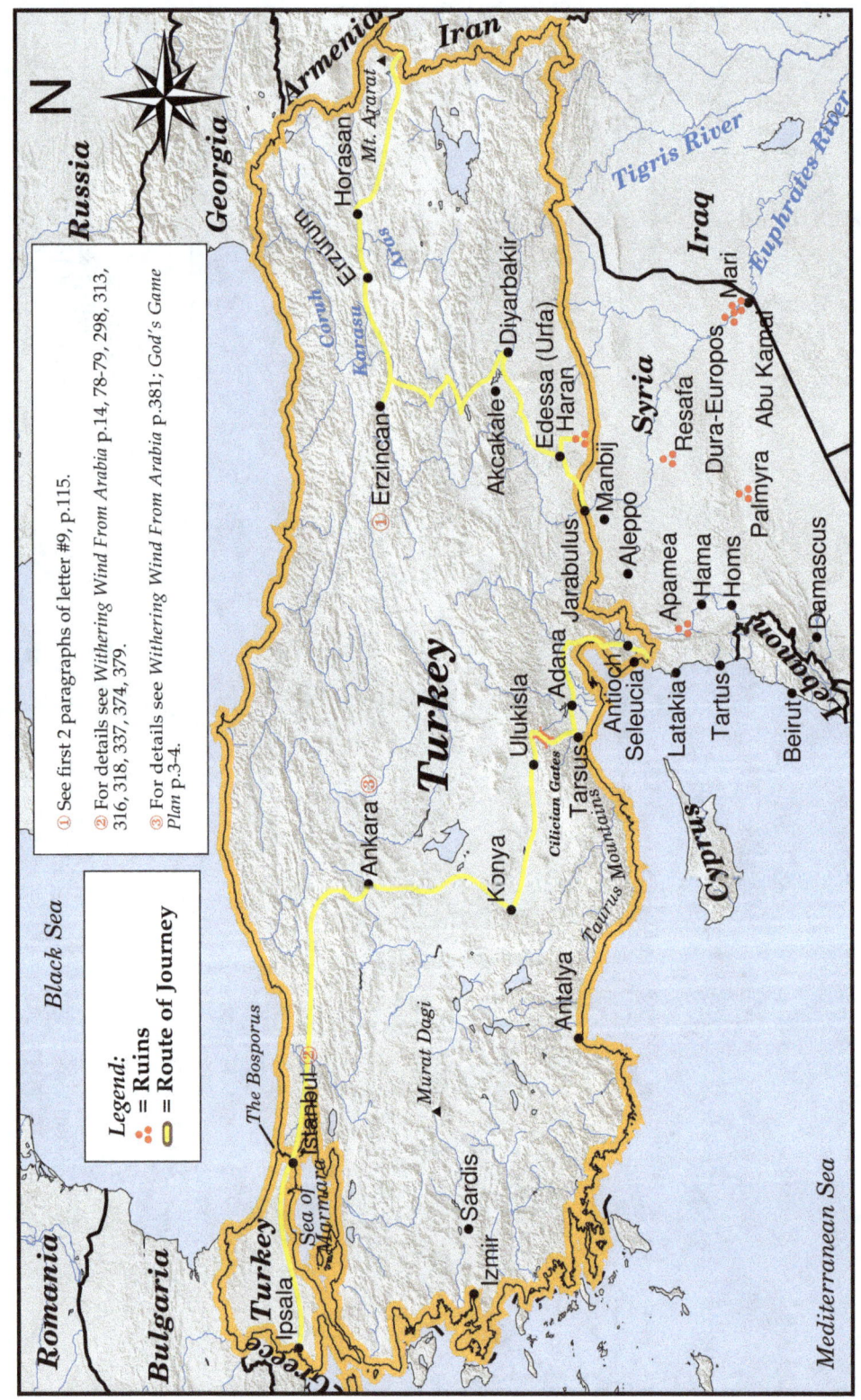

Atlas

Map of Jordan

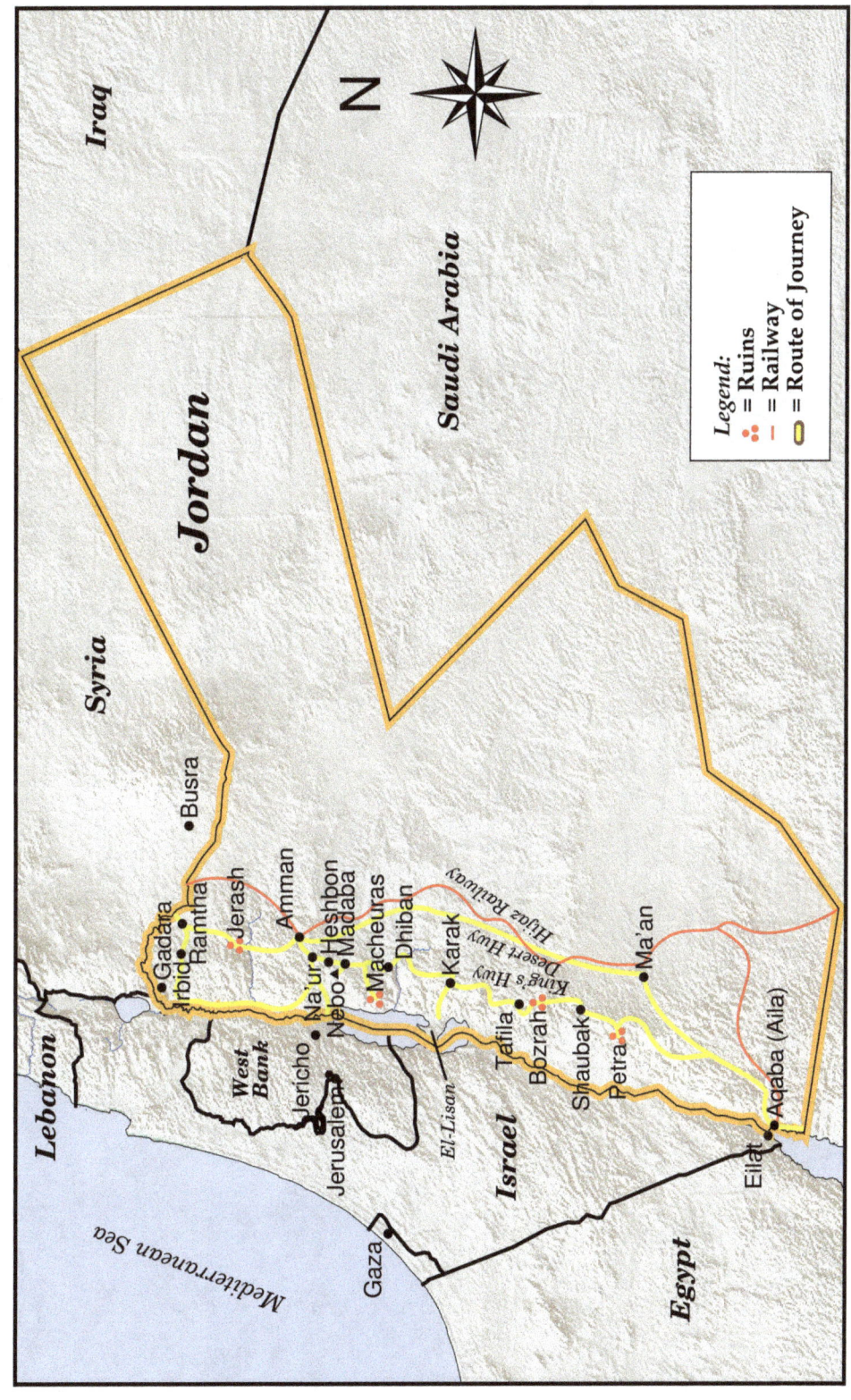

Heartland of the Middle East

MAP OF TURKISH WATERWAYS

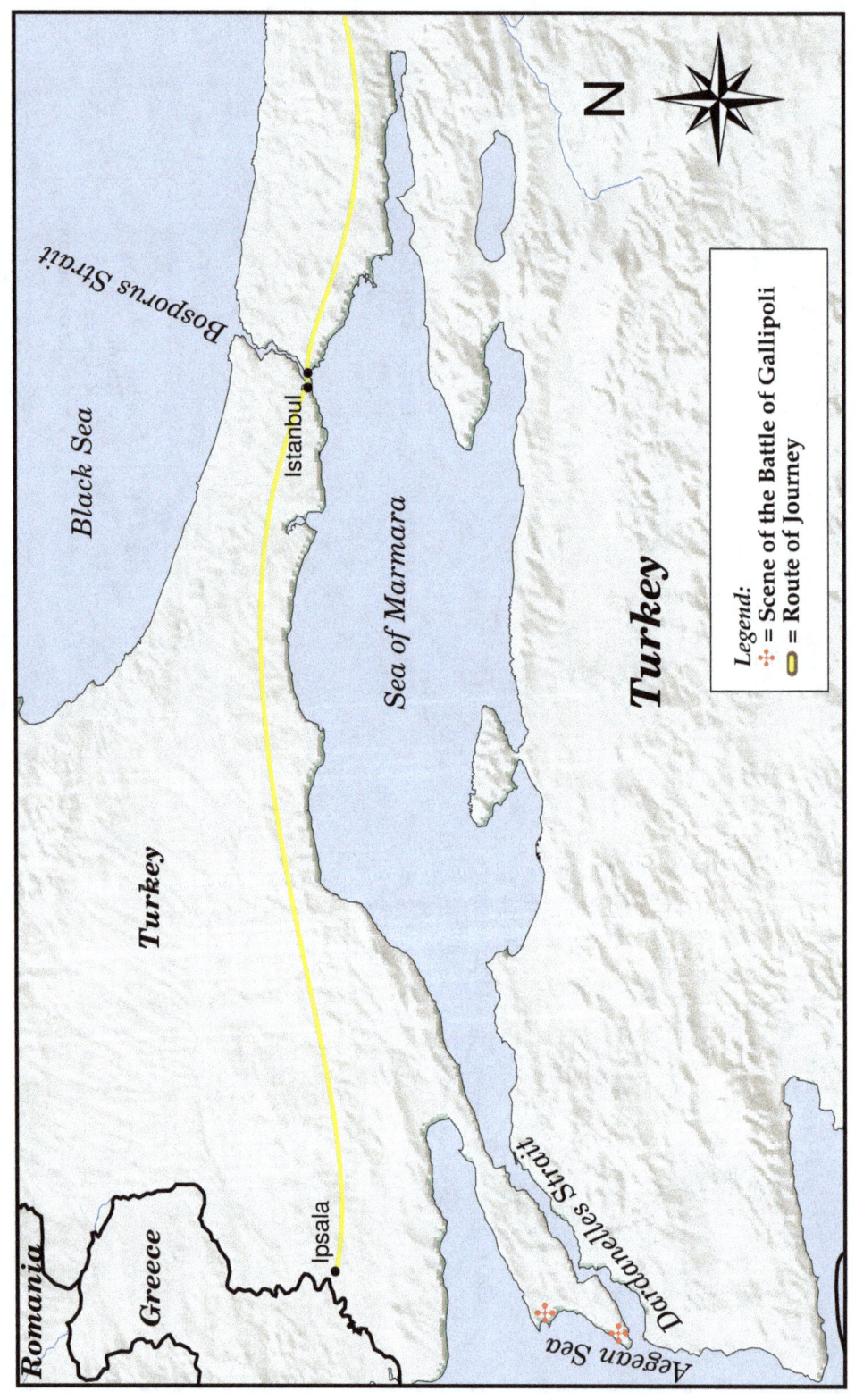

Alphabetical Index

Abadan	110
Abana	145
Abgar, King	129
Abraham	82, 105, 127-130, 139
Abu Kamal	139
Achaemenian	63, 78, 95, 107, 108, 110, 111, 115
Achaemenian Empire	94
Achaemenid	41, 49, 78, 93, 108, 109, 111, 120
Achaemenid Empire	41, 78, 93, 97, 107-111
Achaemenus, King	108, 111
Achmetha	109, 120
Aegean Sea	61, 109, 115
Afghanistan	1, 5-7, 9, 10, 13, 14, 17-23, 25, 27, 29, 33-36, 41, 43, 47, 51, 65, 67, 68
Ahasuerus, King	93, 108, 120
Ahmad Mirza	83
Ahriman	98
Ahwaz	110, 113, 120
Aila	154
Aiyaz	47, 48
Akcakale	131
Al Biruni	48
al-A'way	145
al-Assad, Bashar	95, 169
Al-Hijaz	154
Aleppo	127, 130, 133, 139, 161, 165-167
Alexander the Great	41, 51, 76, 93, 94, 97, 108, 110, 115, 163, 166
Alexander's wall	76
Alla-ud-din Ghori	47
Alptigin	46
Amman	147, 149, 150, 155, 156, 162

Amman Museum	149, 156
Amman-Jerusalem road	161
Ammonite	149
Amol	76
Amorite	139
Amu River	14, 21, 22, 27, 108
Anastasius	134
Anatolia	116
Ansari	48
Anshan	109
Antakya	163
Anti-Lebanon Mountain Range	145, 149
Antioch	4, 41, 85, 86, 163, 164
Antiochus	163
Apame	166
Apamea	4, 164, 166
Aphraat	62
Aqaba	149-152, 154
Arabah	145, 150, 151, 155
Arabia, Roman Province of	154
Arabian Desert	141, 145, 149, 151
Arabic	116, 129, 167
Arachosia	41
Aral Sea	19, 27
Aras	119
Araxes	119
Arghandab River	46
Armenians	82, 88
Artemis	147
Ashoka	38, 42, 43
Ashokan inscriptions	42, 44
Ashurbanipal	106

Alphabetical Index

Asia 1, 13, 17, 18, 21, 25, 28, 41, 49, 63, 115
Asphalt Sea 162
Ataturk, Kemal 115-117
Azerbaidzhan 116
Baal 142
Babol 75
Babolsar 75, 76
Babylon 61, 62, 110, 111, 130, 163
Bacchus 134, 135
Bactria 19, 34
Badakshan Province 27
Baku 116
Balikh River 130
Balkh 14, 19, 46
Bamiyan 10, 33-38, 43
Bamiyan Valley 14, 33, 34, 36, 43, 55
Barada 145
Bashan 145, 147
Bay of Bengal 9
Beas River 108
Beema 135
Begram 28
Behistun 42, 124
Ben Hur 164
Black Sea 61, 115, 119
Bokhara 26
Bosporus 115
Bost 45-47, 49, 68
Bozra 155-157
Britain 22, 64, 125
Buddha 34, 35
Buddhism 6, 7, 10, 14, 34-36, 38, 42

Buddhist	36, 45
Bukhara	18
Burckhardt, Johann Ludwig	155
Buseira	155, 156
Busra	154
Byzantine	85, 115, 135
Byzantium	28
caliphate	115
Carchemish	130, 131
Caspian dialects	73
Caspian Sea	19, 63, 73, 75, 116, 119
cenotaph	109, 122
Central Asia	13, 18, 21, 41, 63
Ch'angan	19
Champollion	124
Chiliarch	77
China	17-19, 25, 28, 34, 36, 42, 51, 63
Choga Zanbil	105-107
City of Weeping	37
Code of Hammurabi	110
Communism	23, 64, 116, 117
Communist Russia	116
Coruh	119
Crown Jewels	76
Cyprus	117
Cyprus issue	117
Cyrus	62, 63, 78, 93, 94, 107-111
Dagon	139
Damascus	26, 119, 130, 131, 139, 145-147, 149, 153, 154, 157
Daniel	25, 41, 47, 94
Daniel's tomb	105
Dante's Inferno	110

Alphabetical Index

Daoud, Mohammad 22, 23
Daphne 164
Dar-ul-Islam 115
Dardanelles 115
Darius 42, 62, 77, 78, 93, 98, 107-110, 121, 124
Darius the Great 62, 77, 78, 109, 124
Daryaoesh 78
Dead Sea 142, 145, 147, 149, 153, 161, 162
Dead Sea Scrolls 142
Decapolis 145, 146, 148
democracy 64
Desert Highway 149, 150, 152, 155
Dez River 73, 105, 107
Dez River Dam 113, 114
Diatessaron 129
Diban 161
Diyarbakir 127
Dunhuang 17
Dur-Untash 106
Dura Synagogue 146
Dura-Europos 119, 137, 146
Ebla 167
Ecbatana 109-111, 163
Edessa 85, 129, 141
Edom 145, 149, 155, 156
Edomites 154, 155
Egypt 9, 78, 131, 153
Eid-us-Zoha 119
Eight-Fold Noble Path 43
El Lisan 145, 161, 162
Elam 62, 104, 105, 109
Elamite 104, 106, 107, 110

Elamite religion	107
Elat	152
Elburz Mountains	73, 76, 77
Elimelech	145
English Channel	63
Epiphanytide	82
Equinox	109
Erzincan	119, 125
Erzurum	125
Esther	120
Ethiopia	61, 95, 108
Euphrates River	10, 85, 86, 105, 110, 111, 119, 130, 131, 133, 138, 167
Europe	27, 34, 51, 63, 115, 119, 167
European	115, 142, 155
Ezion Geber	152, 154
Fars	93, 109
Ferghana Valley	18
Fertile Crescent	130
fez	116
Firdausi	48, 49
Fire Altars	110
Four Noble Truths	43
France	167
Gad	147
Gadara	148
Gadarenes	148
Ganges River	19, 34
Gate of All Nations	109
Gaumata	124
Gaza, Port of	154
Genghis Khan	29, 37, 38, 47
Gerasenes	148

Alphabetical Index

Germany	115
Ghaznavid Dynasty	46
Ghaznavid Empire	19
Ghaznavid Riviera	47
Ghazni	19, 36, 45-47, 49
Ghor	51, 145
Ghorband River	25
Gilead	145, 147
Glueck, Nelson	152
Gondophares	9, 10, 43
Gorgan	73-76
Gorgan River	76
Greece	36, 41, 63, 93, 108, 116, 119, 168
Greeks	23, 30, 41, 93, 111, 115-118, 163, 166
Gujranwala	7
Gulf of Aqaba	145, 151, 154, 157
Haft Tepe	107
Hakim Sanai	48
Hama	164, 165
Hamadan	5, 42, 109, 110, 120-124
Hamath	130, 164
Hammurabi	110, 139
Haran	85, 105, 127-130, 139
Hasa, Wady	147
Hawran	147
Hazarajat	41
Hebrew-Christian community	123
Hellenism	163
Helmand	68
Helmand River	46
Herat	13, 19, 26, 45, 46, 49-51, 67
Herat wind	50, 51

Herat Windmill..50
Heshbon..161
Hijaz Railway..149, 150, 154, 157
Hindu deities..46
Hindu Kush...21, 26, 27, 41
Hindu Kush Mountain Range...21, 25, 34, 41, 44, 51
Hinduism..6, 7
Hitti, Philip K..167
homoneia...166
Homs..119, 145
Horites..154
Hsianfu..19
Hsüan-tsang, Buddhist monk..35, 36
Hussein...95
hypernationalism..29
Hyrcanian Sea..73, 75
Iliad..142
India.............9, 10, 19, 22, 26, 28, 34-36, 38, 41-43, 46, 61, 67, 83, 84, 93, 95, 108
Indian Ocean...19, 21, 61, 64
Indian Subcontinent..46, 64
Indus..3, 4, 61, 109
Indus River...4, 6, 7, 10, 61
Indus River Valley...3, 9, 10, 14, 27
Inshushinak..104, 106
Iran 1, 3, 5, 7, 8, 10, 18, 20-22, 28, 41-43, 49, 61-65, 67-69, 73-76, 81, 82, 84, 85, 88, 93, 95, 107, 108, 119, 126, 167, 169
Iraq..1, 19, 61, 119, 120, 125, 140, 141
Irbid...162
Isfahan...26, 74, 81-84, 88-90, 93, 108, 120
Ishtar..139, 151
Islam..........3, 14, 19, 23, 27, 28, 36, 38, 46, 49, 61, 63, 64, 67, 69, 73, 74, 115-117
Islam Qala..67

Alphabetical Index

Israel 62, 89, 94, 131, 150, 152
Istanbul 116
Izmir 116
Jalal-Din Manguberti 37
Jarabulus 130, 131
Jerash 147, 148
Jericho 156
Jewish-Christian believers 123
Jiza 150
Jordan 119, 121, 145, 149, 150, 152-154, 164
Jordan River 149
Jordan Valley 149, 151
Judaism 89
Julfa 82, 88
Justinian 28, 134
Kabul 21, 22, 25-28, 41, 45, 46, 73, 119, 120
Kakrak 36
Kanishka 34
Kapisa 28
Karak 145, 156, 161
Karun River 82, 105
Kashgar 17
Kashmir 34
Kerala 28
Kermanshah 5, 42
Khiva 21
Khmeimim 167
Khomeini 1, 61
Khomeini Revolution 95
Khorasan 19, 68, 73, 110
Khulm 68
Khuzistan Province 73, 110

King Gondophares	42
king of kings	64
King's Highway	149, 150, 155, 161
Kir of Moab	145
Kirkuk	88
Kirmanshah	120, 122, 124, 125
Kunduz	25, 27, 28, 108
Kurd	125
Kurdistan	125
Kushan	28, 45
Lahore	5, 6, 76, 108
Lake Uramiah	125
Latakia	4, 166, 167
Lawrence of Arabia	146, 149, 157
Lebanon	145, 149, 162
Lebanon Mountain Range	166, 167
Lemberg	123
Lew Wallace	164
Libyan Civil War	169
London	123, 167
lunar calendar	109
Ma'an	149
Machaerus	161, 162
Madaba	161, 162
magi	109
Mahmud of Ghazni	19, 46-49
Maimana	29
Makarios	117
Manasseh	147
Manichaeans	10, 43
Manichaeism	10
Mari	119, 139, 141, 146, 167

Alphabetical Index

Martyn, Henry..108
Mashhad..67, 69, 73, 75, 76
Masjid-e-Soleyman..69, 110
Massoretic text...142
Maximos, Serafim..116
Mecca..116
Media..62, 110, 130
Medina..157
Mediterranean...3, 4, 10, 111, 131, 166, 167, 169
Merv..14, 21
Meshraus..161
Meskenah...133
Mesopotamia..84, 125, 128-130, 138
Micah..62
Middle East...5, 43, 48, 63, 64, 88, 151, 169
Moab..145, 149, 161
Moabite Stone..161, 162
Moabite tradition..145
Moabites...161
Mongol...44
moon worship..128, 130
Mordecai..120
Moses..146, 147, 154, 156
Moslem pilgrimage road...154
Mossadegh..64
Mt. Damavand..76
Mt. Hermon...145
Mu'awiya..129
Mukkawir...161
Murit Dagi..119
Muslim East...116
Mustafa Subhi..116

Na'ur 161, 162
Naaman 145
Nabataeans 154
Nabu-naid 130
Nahor 128, 129, 139
Naomi 145
Naqab Ishtar 151
Naqsh-e-Rustam 83, 120, 121
Nau Roz 109
Nebo 162
Nebuchadnezzar 61, 62, 131
Neco 131
Nestorian Controversy 86
Nile 131
Nisibis 85
North Africa 115, 169
Orontes River 10, 163, 164, 166, 167
Orontes River Valley 151, 166
Ottoman Empire 117
Ottomans 81, 115, 116
Oxus River 13, 14, 19, 21, 27, 63
paganism 130
Pakistan 3-8, 10, 21, 22, 28, 43, 64, 67, 68, 93, 108, 119, 167
Palestine 9, 130, 156
Palmyra 119, 133, 137-142, 152, 154
Pamir Mountains 27, 63
Pars 61, 93
Parsee 93
Parthia 62
Parthian 19
Parthian Empire 9, 18, 133, 154
Pasargadae 93-95, 107-109, 111, 120

Alphabetical Index

Pashtunistan..22, 65
Persepolis...........................61, 77, 94-96, 103, 107, 109-111, 120, 121, 142, 166
Persia...10, 19, 28, 34, 36, 46, 48, 61, 62, 123
Persian Empire..110, 130
Persian Gulf..65, 75, 110, 154
Persians...62, 93, 115, 130, 139, 141
Peshawar..6, 7, 28
Petra...152-155
Pharpar...145
pilgrimage..35
Purim..122
Qandahar...36, 41, 43, 45, 49
Quetta..43
Qum...120
Rabbah..149
Rabbath-Ammon..145, 149
Radio Israel..131
railway..149, 150
Rajputana Desert..19
Ramtha...147
Raqqa...130
Ras en Naqab..151
Ras Shamra..4
Rashadiya...155
Rawalpindi...6, 7
Rawlinson..124
reclining Buddha..46
Red Sea..146, 151-154
Red Sea Port..152
Ressafa..133, 134, 137, 138
Reuben..147
Revived Islam..116

Rezaiah	125
Rezeph	133, 137
Rhine	62
Rift Valley	151
Roman	153
Roman Empire	62, 63, 86, 141
Romans	83, 85, 115, 138, 154
Rome	18, 25, 28, 34, 36, 62, 63, 86, 141, 153, 154
Russia	9, 20-22, 27, 34, 63, 75, 116, 117, 167, 169
Safavid	82, 84
Salang Pass	26, 33
Salang Tunnel	21, 27
Salten Sea	162
Samangan	68
Samarkand	18, 21, 30
sarcophagus	94, 109
Sardis	108, 163
Sassania	18, 19, 62, 85, 86, 88, 125, 139
Sassanian	18, 19, 62, 85, 86, 88, 125, 139
Sassanian Empire	18, 36, 85, 86
satellite-tracking facility	127
Saudi Arabia	152, 157
SAVAK	61
scroll of The Law	122
Sea of Marmara	115
Seistan	9, 14
Seleucia	163
Seleucid Empire	41, 85, 138, 166
Seleucus Nicator	41, 85, 115, 138, 163, 164, 166
Seljuks	115, 116
Selucia-Ctesiphon	86
Semiretchi	13

Alphabetical Index

Seraphim 77
Sergiopolis 134
Sergius 134, 135
Shah 64
Shah Abbas 83, 84, 88
Shaubak 155
Sher Khan Bandar 27
Shia Muslims 74
Shibar Pass 33
Shiraz 93, 104, 108-110, 120
Shush 104, 105
Shushan 78, 93, 104, 111
sig 154
Silk Road 4, 17, 25, 28, 34
Sind 19
Sinkiang Province 17
Sistan 9
Soboktagin 36, 38
Sogdians 18
Solomon 94, 141
Soviet Union 20-23, 64, 116, 117
Strait of Gibraltar 115
stupa 36
Suez 65
Suez Canal 157
Suleiman 81
Susa 78, 104, 106-110, 119, 120
Syr River 9
Syria 9, 10, 41, 85, 95, 119, 125, 127, 131, 133, 137, 138, 145, 149, 153, 161, 162, 164, 165, 167, 169
Syriac 17, 18, 129, 139
Tabriz 108, 125

Tadmor	137, 141
Tafila	155
Taliban	35
Tamerlane	9, 26, 82
Tapa Sardar	45
Tarikh-e Tabari	38
Tarim Desert	18
Tartus	167
Taxila	10
Tayebad	67
Tehran	64, 73, 75, 76, 78, 119, 120, 123
Terah	128, 129, 139
Thomas	9, 10, 13, 43, 44
Tien Shan Mountain	17
Tigris River	105, 111, 163
Tigris-Euphrates Valley	139
tomb of Cyrus	94
Tongue, The	161
Tophel	155
Trajan	154
Trajan, Emperor	153
Transoxiana	19
Treaty of Lausanne	116
Treaty of Sevres	116
Trojan war	142
Turfan	17
Turkestan	21
Turkey	115-117, 119, 125-127, 129, 131, 157, 163, 164, 169
Turks	36, 115-117
Tus	49
Ugarit	167
Unai-Hajigak Pass	33

Alphabetical Index

Untash Gal..106
Ur..105, 128
Urfa..129, 130
Urhai..129
Urumchi...17
Uyghur Muslims..17
Vienna, Austria..81
Wadi Araba..153
Wady Hasa..147
Wady Karak...145
Wallace, Lew...164
World War I...17, 115, 116, 149, 157, 167
World War II...22, 29, 64
Xerxes..77, 93, 107, 120
Zagros Mountains...110
Zayandehrud River..82, 90
Zenobia, Queen..137, 141
Zered River..147
ziggurat..105-107
Zoroastrian...63, 109, 110

Heartland of the Middle East

ABOUT THE AUTHOR

After 15 years of ministry in Pakistan, toward the end of 1975, the author and his family were no longer allowed to renew their residential visas and consequently had to terminate their on-site mission work in Pakistan. On their way back to America, Lee and Jonathan, his youngest son, traveling by Jeep, made a six-month study-tour of the Middle East. It included Afghanistan, Iran, Turkey, Jordan and Syria. During that tour Lee sent a series of letters home entitled *Travel Letters From the Center Arena of History* which have evolved into this book.

The author graduated from San Jose Bible College with a Bachelor of Theology Degree in 1947. In 1956, after having served nine-and-one-half years in evangelistic Christian ministry at Vancouver, Washington, and having taught four years in a Portland, Oregon-based Bible college, he entered the graduate school of the University of Pennsylvania, where in 1959 he completed his M.A. Degree in South Asia Regional Studies. His thesis was *A Contribution to the English Historical Cartography of Iran in the Early Islamic Period.*

Following the completion of his studies at the University of Pennsylvania, he and his family sailed to Pakistan in August 1960 where they spent the next fifteen years in Christian evangelism, both urban and rural. For a short time during the early part of his stay in Pakistan, he also studied history and political science at the University of the Punjab in Lahore, Pakistan.

While living in Pakistan, Turner made several study and preaching trips to various sites throughout much of India. Also, due to a war between India and Pakistan in 1971, he and his family spent six months in Afghanistan during which he became acquainted with further aspects of that country's history, geography and current condition. After 1975, Lee made 22 trips back to Pakistan and several additional trips to India. As a board member of IDES, a U.S. Christian relief organization, he visited Sudan and Egypt several times. Also, in India he traveled to war-torn Imphal in the remote, far northeastern corner of that great country, to help implement relief projects.

While still in Pakistan, the Turners began a shortwave radio outreach in the Urdu language in order to reach more people with the message of Christ. Those broadcasts have continued uninterruptedly and go out under the name of *Awaz-e-Haq (The Voice of Truth)*. The work has expanded so that the programs can also be heard worldwide on internet radio, available 24/7. The ministry is carried on by a small group of dedicated and skilled brethren under the name of Key Communications and is directed by Jonathan Turner.

For additional information, see www.keycom.org.

www.ingramcontent.com/pod-product-compliance
Lightning Source LLC
Chambersburg PA
CBHW080732230426
43665CB00020B/2717